Voices & Visions
of the
American West

VOICES & VISIONS

OF THE AMERICAN ✳ ★ WEST

Photographed and Edited by Barney Nelson

Introduction by Elmer Kelton

★

TexasMonthlyPress

Texas Monthly Press, Inc.
P.O. Box 1569
Austin, Texas 78767

A B C D E F G H

Library of Congress Cataloging-in-Publication Data

Nelson, Barney, 1947-
Voices & visions of the American West.

1. Cowboys—West (U.S.)—Pictorial works.
2. Cowboys—West (U.S.)—Miscellanea. 3. West (U.S.)
—Social life and customs—Pictorial works. 4. West
(U.S.)—Social life and customs—Miscellanea.
I.   Title. II.   Title: Voices and visions of the
American West.
F596.N42   1986   978   86-5962
ISBN 0-87719-049-6

Book design by Whitehead & Whitehead
Printed in Japan by Dai Nippon Printing Co. Ltd.
through DNP (America), Inc.

Frontispiece: Moving the remuda, 06 Ranch, Alpine, Texas.

Colophon: 06 Ranch, Alpine, Texas.

DEDICATION

Twenty years ago Boots, Emma and Wendell Guest took on an eighteen-year-old, rodeo-style, phony cowgirl and put her horseback to help work the rough, brushy Triangle M Ranch near Mayer, Arizona. It could have been called a greasy sack outfit except the hard-riding owners couldn't afford bacon to grease the sack.

Worse than worthless, monopolizing the use of a good horse, the girl left a trail of hide and cloth clinging to manzanita and oak brush just trying to keep their dust in sight. When a twig snapped on the Triangle M, there were an uneasy few seconds for her to decide whether to try to pursue or escape.

Wendell tried to teach her how to stay alive and how to quench her thirst by chewing tobacco. Emma taught her that only a woman was tough enough to ride from dark to dark and serve hot biscuits for supper. She also taught her to pull the tarp over her head to keep the rats out of her bed at night. Boots taught her to judge people by when and why they pull up.

Sunburnt, bloody and bone-weary, her reward for a job not well done but finished, was a cowboy baptism by Wendell and a burly friend. Carried kicking and screaming to the creek, she was doused with icy water, sand and a new name: Jake. That was twenty years ago. The Triangle M is now the weekend toy of a Phoenix businessman. Boots, Emma and Wendell don't bend hell down bouldered creekbeds anymore, but Jake—now called Barney—still has a fingernail hold on the life they taught her to love. The name didn't stick. But the baptism did.

I hope this book stirs some good memories for the first three real cowboys I ever tried to follow.

Love,

JAKE

CONTENTS

PREFACE

FIFTEEN YEARS AGO I discovered that my words and photographs would sell, although I hope no one goes back and looks up any of that early work to read. It's sort of like having a photographer around on your first cowboy job. People will always assume that you still sit a horse the same way. Printer's ink is very permanent. It doesn't wash off and once it gets into your bloodstream, it is there to stay. My good friend Gary Morton, the former wagon boss of New Mexico's Bell Ranch, said, "Once cowboying is in your blood it's there to stay." Evidentally I suffer from both diseases: cowboying and publishing.

Last spring a pretty young girl walked up to me at the Jordan Valley Oregon Big Loop Rodeo and asked, "How can I get a job like yours?" I just stood there looking at her with my mouth open. Answers swam around in my head like "What job?" or "Shoot up thousands of dollars worth of film and then you'll be ready to sell one photograph for $100." I'm not sure I ever answered her. I probably just stared until she got frightened and left the scene. But her question still haunts me.

Perhaps more than any other subject, the cowboy has been raped and plundered. Hollywood, television, Western pulp novels, country songs, clothes manufacturers—and the list goes on and on. Some people think it's easy to become an expert on the subject of cowboys: just add a little fringe here and there, put a little uneducated twang into the language, get horseback and you got it. In theory, any good New York photographer can photograph him and any good San Francisco writer can tell his story. But I don't think so.

The public is finally sophisticated enough to realize that most cowboys, even in a hurry, don't hop on their horses over the cantle. But Western wear companies still publish slick four-color ads where the model has his spurs on upside down.

We have filled libraries, yet we are no closer to understanding the man under the hat than we were a hundred years ago. I once thought that the boss simply surrounded a bunch of cattle with cowboys and they would automatically go in the pens. Then someone stuck a branding iron against their hide and that was about it. Now I know that what kind of metal an iron is made of makes a difference—how the vents are cut and how it is heated. A brand can be clean or blotched depending on how the animal is held, how hot the iron is, how thick the hair, how wet, how the brander holds the iron, and what color the skin is. Surrounding cattle with a bunch of cowboys is a science and an art that would take more pages than any publisher could afford to print.

Every moment of a cowboy's day is filled with subtleties, and no one ever learns them all. A very fine line determines being in the right place at the right time. Yes, how did I get this unpaid job as a spokesman for cowboys, and who gave it to me? No one did, I took it. And a good rule to follow around cowboys when you don't know what you are doing is to just try to stay out of the way. That's what I've tried to do, stay out of the way. I've tried to let the cowboys speak for themselves for a change. Instead of orchestrating the photographs, I've tried to stay out of the way and let my subjects set the stage in their own ways.

I'm not sure how much success I've had but the quest has been a good one. It's like the old queston, "Are you a real cowboy?" And the old traditional answer: "No, but maybe I'll do until one comes along."

ACKNOWLEDGMENTS

T HIS BOOK would still be a dream if it hadn't been for people who were there when I needed them most: Ray and Carolyn Hunt, John and Winnie Latta, Waddie and Tootie Mitchell, David Moore, Elmer Kelton, Gary and Suzie Morton, Mike and Susan Stephens, Tom and Sue Moorhouse, and the Dugan Wagon crew. They were never too busy or too tired. They always said what I needed when I needed it—good or bad. In spite of my own doubts, they believed in me and somehow made me believe too.

Many photographs and words used have been or will be printed in such magazines as *Western Horseman, The Cattleman, The Quarter Horse Journal, Texas Hereford, Texas Monthly, Horse and Rider, Arabian Horse World, GEO,* and *L'Espresso.* To busy editors such as Randy Witte at *Western Horseman,* who dug through files and returned photographs that hadn't even been published yet, I will be forever grateful.

Thanks to Alpine Travel for patiently getting me somehow from one obscure place to the next and to Kathy Marcus at *Texas Monthly* magazine for the push, and to Colleen Watt who proofread for me while her husband helped mine work cattle.

Thanks to people pictured in this book and even more to those whose words I use either from interviews or letters. People who don't know you will judge you by them, and you know it. I hope I've done you justice.

Finally, thanks a lot to my daughter, Carla, and to the man who made our saddles and most of our gear, who assigns and shoes our horses, and who handles the embarrassment of being married to a damn photographer very well.

06 Ranch, Alpine, Texas.

INTRODUCTION

ALL OVER THE WORLD, people know the cowboy, or believe they do. Traveling in Europe, wearing even a modest LBJ-style hat, I have caught the attention of adults and have been followed by children whispering speculations about the cowboy. The cowboy has become so much a symbol that the reality behind him has largely been lost except among those who know him.

Even those of us who know him let ourselves be distracted sometimes by the legend more than we would want to admit.

Many people view the cowboy as a romantic, exotic figure bigger than life, almost like something out of Sir Walter Scott's stories of chivalry and knighthood. On the other hand, his detractors declare him just another hired hand who happens to spend part of his time on horseback, his existence grubby, menial and generally unpleasant. At either extreme he borders on the mythical.

I have been around the cowboy all my life and but for a general ineptitude at the trade, might be one myself. To me he has always represented a little of both the images I have cited but also a great deal that is neither.

My people were cowboys for three generations before I came along, and some of my own generation—though not I—have maintained the working cowboy tradition. One of my great-grandfathers was a cattleman in the Indian Territory and later in Central Texas. Another left deep East Texas more than a century ago with a covered wagon and a string of horses to move west and take up land in Callahan County. My paternal grandfather grew up punching cattle, breaking horses and mules, and spent his life on West Texas ranches. My father under his tutelage became a cowboy, later a ranch foreman and finally a general manager. His life, from beginning to end, was centered around cattle and horses.

As a boy on the McElroy Ranch in Upton and Crane counties of West Texas, I was only dimly aware that any world existed other than that of cowboys and cattlemen until I became seven years old and started to school among youngsters whose fathers worked principally in the oil patch. I did not know there was supposed to be something extraordinary about the cowboy, that so many people had all these fanciful ideas so different from the reality around me.

Then and now, I have seen the cowboy principally in terms of his work and his environment. Having lived in the midst of his kind through my formative years, and still exposed to his influence much of the time, I believe I know him pretty well.

The cowboy of the romantic image spends a lot of his day sitting around on a pretty horse and looking picturesque. He never seems to associate with cows very much, except that now and then he is seen driving a large and colorful herd in which no cripples are evident, no spoiled-bag cows, no runty calves that need shipping at the owner's first convenience.

The cowboy I knew in my youth was above all good at what he did, and he worked hard at it. He had to, to hold a job. When I was a boy, the ranches knew no such thing as a labor shortage. A man "made a hand" or was soon replaced by someone who did. The days tended to be long, usually starting by daylight if not sooner. My father had an inexplicable habit of getting us up to milk the cow and eat breakfast in the pitch black of early morning, take us on horseback to the far side of the big pasture, then sit and wait there an hour for the sun to rise so we could see the cattle we were going to round up. Workdays often did not end until dusk, or even full dark. The job was often hot—or painfully cold—gritty and sometimes most uncomfortable. It was hard to look or feel glamorous while flanking calves in the blistering summer heat and the choking dust of a branding pen, or doctoring bloody wounds of cattle infested by screwworms, or repeatedly bucking off a jugheaded horse that made his own declaration of independence.

Nevertheless, most of the cowboys I ever knew had a quiet pride in their occupation and in their individual skills that enabled them to live up to its exacting demands. To a degree, no doubt, they themselves became influenced by the romantic image and made an effort to live up to it. I remember many who gave it up for the higher pay of the oilfields or other work. Some came back to it, after a time, glad to be "home" again. Others never did, but they would visit the ranch when special "cow works" were underway. They liked to watch, perhaps to pitch in and help, to relive for a little while, a lifestyle they had put behind them for a better paycheck, usually more for the comfort of their families than for their own.

As demanding as it might have been at times, as unpleasant as it could be when the weather or the animals went against them, as meagerly as it always paid for the time and sweat and skill invested, they retained an affection for the cowboy life that was stronger than I have seen for other occupations.

I have known a lot of ex-cowboys who went into other professions, often earning many times more money and building an estate they could never have accomplished from the hurricane deck of a cow pony. Yet, often they have told me that the high point of their lives was the time they worked on such-and-such a ranch, twenty or thirty or forty miles from town, earning thirty or fifty or seventy-five dollars a month. To be sure, they relied on a selective memory which called up the more agreeable aspects of that life, but always there seemed to be enough of those to justify the hard knocks, the interminable working days, the risks that derived from pitting themselves against half-wild cattle and half-wild horses determined to cripple or kill them. There was always an unstated but obvious satisfaction in standing up to their peers, in being able to catch more cattle with fewer loops or successfully ride a bronc that had thrown off some other respected hand.

Barney Nelson is at home in the Big Bend country, a challenging land of many big ranches. Some still work cattle much in the same manner as they did fifty or seventy-five years ago. In much of the ranching industry, modern technology has erased many oldtime challenges, replacing them with methods safer and more efficient for the company but not half so much fun. The cowboy finds himself spending more of his day in a pickup or on a tractor than a-horseback. His hands may toughen more on a welding unit than on a rope. The tiny tallybook my father used to carry in his shirt pocket—almost his only venture into bookkeeping—may be replaced by a detailed set of records on birth and weaning weights, pickup mileage and time spent on various of the ranch's designated "profit centers" so the company computer can sort out those which do indeed return a profit. All too often, it finds that the cattle do not.

Barney Nelson's cowboys and cowgirls are well acquainted with the modern touches and may even embrace a lot of them. But they also reflect old values and old ways not yet lost, or at least not yet forgotten. They tend to reflect a touch of romance that has little to do with the Hollywood legend but rather the cowboy's own vision of himself and his life. Their recollections, which make up most of this book's text, reflect a certain glory in the challenges, a wry humor in recalling incidents not funny at the time but hilarious in retrospect, once the danger was past and the consequences met.

Lest readers suspect Barney of "doctoring up" these accounts, let me say that most of the cowboys I ever knew were natural storytellers. My father never wrote anything longer than a family letter, but he was a match for the best of raconteurs when sitting around a campfire or on a bunkhouse porch. As a youngster I spent many a pleasant hour trying to be inconspicuous while Dad and the cowhands swapped yarns, often well past my bedtime. They talked mostly of their workaday world, of appalling "jackpots" into which rough stock had swept them. They talked of horses either very good or very bad, both kinds held in certain reverence.

They judged other men mostly by their cowboy skills, not by their possessions or positions in society. They could look down on a wealthy landowner who could have bought with his pocket change everything the cowboy owned but who did not know how to trip a steer. Yet they could exalt a rogue who was good on horseback. I remember a locally notorious puncher regarded by his peers as a con artist of the highest magnitude; they took a deep hold on their wallets when they saw him riding in. But they respected him, for they could overlook a few minor personal faults in a man who was a top hand with cattle and horses.

It takes a lot more than the costume to make a cowboy, and the costume falsely worn will not long fool those who know the breed. A real cowboy is a highly skilled technician in a field where textbooks offer little help. The best are born into the work. It is difficult for someone already grown to maturity to take up the cowboy trade and ever develop the proficiency of those who grew up in it, learning at their fathers' sides by example as much as by direction. Learning to outguess a cow or a horse is not a skill easily articulated or taught; it is absorbed by osmosis and by long years of observation, trial and error.

It has always been a major regret of my life that I was never able to achieve enough skill to call myself a cowboy. When I went out to help, it was as if two able men had saddled up and ridden away. No amount of honors won in any other occupation will ever totally make up for that disappointment.

After all I have said about the practical and realistic side of the cowboy life, I must admit to some addiction to the romantic side of it as well. When I was about four years old we lived in a ranch linecamp in the Crane County sandhills. A scene that has remained vivid in my memory was a cattle herd spilling down the side of a shinnery-speckled dune and into the big open corrals, my father on horseback behind them. I have never seen a picture more striking, and I know I never shall, though I have been searching ever since.

Barney Nelson has also been searching, and she has found what she was looking for. We are fortunate that she has shared the images with us.

ELMER KELTON
San Angelo, Texas

Voices & Visions
of the
American West

CHAPTER ONE

ROMANCE

Like most romances it all begins with
physical attraction.

ONE WINTER MORNING I sat in a cozy cafe drinking coffee with a seasoned old rancher. Without much conversation, we watched a fierce January storm raging outside, blowing dry, icy snow across the parking lot like dust. "Just look at that weather," he said, "I bet nobody's out in it but cowboys and dogs." But instead of pity, I sensed a little envy in his voice. Another cowboy-turned-gentleman-rancher once told me of a time when he was caught camped on roundup during the worst rain and hailstorm of West Texas history. They were drenched, their beds were soaked, and the rain washed away the cook's fire and their supper. What he remembered best, though, were the waterfalls pouring off the rimrock above them in great spouts.

One of my favorite cowboys once said, "Every now and then you ride out on a rim or down a canyon and the fog is rolling in or the sun is hitting a bluff just right, and it makes you wonder if anybody else ever saw it just that way." That same cowboy was camped on a mountaintop the night the Northern Lights made a great red show across Texas skies. Few others saw it, too many being blinded by television and neon. Riding through a lightning storm on the flats or caught out after dark by moonrise—no, no one but the cowboy has ever seen it just that way. Contained herein are some beautiful moments, but the best and rarest are never seen by photographers, rich folks or even presidents. Those very special moments that come around only once in a lifetime are reserved for the cowboys and dogs. Show me a cowboy who isn't doing this at least partly for the romance, and I'll show you a cowboy who's only in it for the money.

I never met a rich man who didn't want to be a cowboy or a rancher.

ALBERTO MUZQUIZ, *Rancher*
Rancho La Rosita
Muzquiz, Coahuila, Mexico

Twenty years ago cowboys were just more or less doing a job, and it wasn't so cosmetic as it is now. I don't think it's ruined it, but I don't think it's helped. Things are easier now. People have more transportation now. They go to town more, they get around. They don't work like they used to and wages are not real good for this inflation, but they're better than they used to be. It's a hard way to put it, but it's true. Take all these young fellows—they're all good people and it's not their fault, but they've been indoctrinated to think they've got more coming quicker than what they've really got coming. Yeah, cowboys have changed. I can't say better, I can't say worse.

ROYCE HANSON, *Cowboss*
JD Ranch
Carlin, Nevada

Our office is full of bright, young, college-educated professionals. Their methods seem to be—do it quickly, the easiest way, and don't worry about correctness (either technically or morally) and hope to make a good impression and move on before the results are evaluated. The old way of life is vanishing in places other than the ranch.

HARRY D. HILDENBRAND
Marketing Representative
Pittsburgh, Pennsylvania

Up to five years ago I buckarooed in eastern Nevada at some smaller places, nothing as large as the IL or YP. I did it to get through school in the summer when I was at Texas A&M getting my B.S. I never had too many opportunities to get pictures of that way of life

Montana.

which I really miss. Now a chemical engineer working my way through Yale trying to become a Ph.D. in biochemical engineering, I feel maybe I should have stayed out there and not have grown up. When I get depressed from the rat race up here, I look at cowboy pictures and it brings me back to life. One day soon I hope I'll be able to go back to the cow country, God willing maybe to visit or even work again. But for now I should finish school.

MARK A. SIMON
Biochemical Engineer
New Haven, Connecticut

I'm a young man who wants to work on a ranch during my holidays. Last year I spent two weeks on a "real working cattle ranch" in Arizona, but it wasn't really that kind of ranch. Just 300 head of cattle and nothing to do. More a dude ranch for people who want to play cowboy. I want to work with the cowboys, to share all the time with these guys. I can ride, will bring my own saddle, and I can work hard and long. But I also must say I cannot rope, because I haven't a chance to work cattle here in old Germany.

WILLI OSTIADAL
Munich, West Germany

Texas.

Texas.

A friend and I were driving down the highway up near Gruver, in the northern Texas Panhandle. The temperature was right around ten degrees—and had been for about four days—and we came upon a cowboy pushing some cows down a fence row. Without a doubt, he had on all the clothes he could get into, but he was wearing his hat—no cap. He did have a wild rag covering his ears and most of his face, but you could see the frost on the outside of the scarf, just as the horse's whiskers were covered with frost. As we passed the man my friend said, "Anybody who thinks they want to be a cowboy ought to ride with him just one day."

JIM JENNINGS, *Assistant Editor and Editorial Director*
The Quarter Horse Journal
Amarillo, Texas

When Roy Rogers was big a lot of guys grew up looking up to him, thinking that's what the cowboy was. That wasn't exactly true. That wasn't the real thing. Now I think a lot of these young guys look at the *Western Horseman* and all the publicity these cowboys get, and it's the same thing. It's the same idea. But a true, genuine cowboy is a lot different than a lot of these magazines and books show. These young guys, they need to get out around some good, successful cowboys to find out what a true cowboy is. They can't just read the *Western Horseman* and look at Charlie Russell's pictures and come out here and be a cowboy. It takes years of experience—experience around good cowboys.

MARTIN BLACK, *Buckaroo*
Gamble Ranch
Montello, Nevada

Many times the more they try to look the buckaroo image, the less help they are. The more gaudy they are, seems like, the less they are. You can just tell by looking, after a while. You get used to seeing people and working with them. The more conservative they look, it seems like, the better help they are. People that are ranch-raised look different from people that want to be cowboys but have been raised differently.

BRYAN NEUBERT, *Buckaroo*
Robert R. Marvel Ranches
Lamoille, Nevada

Mom bought me a Hopalong Cassidy suit and a pair of Roy Rogers guns when I was a kid. I rode my grandfather's horse, but it wasn't until I was twenty when I married Sharon and we bought a couple of horses that I started riding regularly.

J. SHARRELL BURCHAM, *Foreman*
Cowan Cattle Company
Big Sandy, Montana

You'd be surprised at the number of people that think we still carry guns out here and that we're not civilized. A lot of people don't realize what's involved out here, what the life is like. They think that a ranch might have four or five cows. They can't visualize the scope of it, how big it is—and that it is still basically the same as it was.

BIT ROBERTSON, *Cowboy*
Alpine, Texas

Idaho.

Ever since I was a little old kid I wanted to be a cowboy. I grew up there around Fort Worth, and I was pretty much of a cowboy because I had a hat and a horse and a pair of boots. I got a little older and that wasn't quite good enough. So I started rodeoing and then I was sure enough a cowboy. I was the North Texas High School Rodeo Association champion bull rider one year and at the same time was also working at the branding chutes of the Fort Worth stockyards, so that made me a real cowboy. I had a chance to go to Moran and work on a ranch out there. And I figured there weren't many cowboys out there so I'd go help them out—and thought I'd show them something. So after I got out there I found out that they were the ones that were showing me something, and I finally figured out that rodeoing wasn't cowboying and that sure-enough cowboying was what I was wanting to do.

Oregon.

Well, I got to be a cowboy there at Moran. Eventually I left there and went a little farther west and found out again that I wasn't a cowboy. I learned a little more there and moved on to another ranch. I thought I was a cowboy by then but worked there a little while and figured out I wasn't. I finally ended up in Alpine and started working on the Catto-Gage Ranch and found out again that I *still* wasn't a cowboy. But I finally figured out that if I'd shut up and kind of watch, I might learn something. So here I am now at the U Up and U Down and I guess I still ain't no cowboy, but I have learned to shut up a little bit.

RANDY GLOVER, *Cowboss*
U Up and U Down Ranch
Fort Davis, Texas

COWBOY SIGN

With the study of pages, written down through the ages
That have brought the cowboy fame,
It will be no mystery, if we go down in history
As being all one and the same.

We're portrayed with the visions of trail dust and horizons
Indistinguished as we gallop in stride.
But in the cow-handler's society, there's as great a variety
As there is in the ranges we ride.

And we all have our tests, we think make us the best
So without intending to rile,
My poem will now roam, to where I call home,
And I'll brag a bit of our style.

Now there's an army about, to hold 'em up and head 'em out,
To ride point and the drag and the flank.
But when all that is seen, is deep tracks and thin green,
It requires the heads of the rank.

And a jillion world-beaters, on the mechanical cheaters
That haul 'em and maul 'em and squeeze;
But a skill is in need, when it's just man and his steed
And they're ringing faraway trees

It's been spoke of for eons and glorified in bronze,
As seen from the fringe in a trot.
So I'll have to be content to try to document
How it looks from the blood and the snot.

The art has no schools, and no book of rules
But one I was told to master,
When my mount was led outside, and I stepped astride
With a hand on the seat of my diaper.

Now I had a big edge in toppin' over that ridge
That very few kids ever had,
For a monument to stand for the wild-cow land,
The statue would include my dad.

If man has shown how to find and conquer the cow,
The example he could be.
And no one's took a crack at trying to follow his track,
Who could ever disagree.

We've served the cloven-hoof critter on the Gila River
And the Pedro where they join in the dell,
Among the spines and the damps, and Satan's line camps
Too rough for headquarters of Hell.

If country can be had that will let 'em be bad,
We have it all in place.
And the results at day's end will always depend
On how we performed in the chase.

Now I've been told of brave deeds by other cowboy breeds
That they handled with ease, of course.
But I've wilder stories to tell about some of the hell
I've had in wrangling the wrangle horse.

If you doubt my right to talk this fight,
Well, boys, I've paid the toll.
From the sweat below to the numbin' snow,
Where the wild bull-bellers roll.

Thinned the cactus flat and slapped the mountain's hat,
I've stood the trials of dread,
And cast my rope with skill or hope
At about every shape of head.

Swam the chilling roars, with tough leading chores,
Hours after last of sun,
And played a hunch with the rankest bunch,
And hit the trap with every one.

Sloshed through sand and mud, till I spit up blood
On foot in the river hairs.
And my heart has stopped, when one limb popped
Where the old loners make their lairs.

Jumped inbred bovines of no telling what bloodlines,
In roughest of canyon heads,
And tripped the seeds of the pedigreeds
In deep ground-dweller beds.

Trailed the outlawed ox, through the devil's box,
Where before no sign had been.
And swore in hock-deep bogs, with tired horse and no dogs,
And slim chance to ever win.

Texas.

Broke to clean air, and the high-noon glare,
From the thicket's musty night;
And the open run, where I've hooked a ton
With not a stirrup-high bush in sight.

Heard the necked up stag rip the lone cedar snag,
Far from his now-lost herd,
And we've carried on talks, by lighting sotol stalks
And understood every word.

Stopped the maverick's flight at the start of night,
To find my flints were drenched,
And seen the bone-deep ooze and missing number twos,
As our saddles we uncinched.

Made all the right dives on the toughest of drives,
Then proudly I could think,
And choked the bad-horned steer, with the shame of fear,
Aboard a blowing, spraddled dink.

Coaxed shelly range kings, snugged up through my D-rings,
Sitting tall through the tired and hurts;
And rolled from belly flops in the cold smelly slops,
Bogged up to my saddle skirts.

Got bad bunches stopped, milled and hammerlocked,
Then to rasp their bouncing feet;
We've rimmed 'em high, where no cowchips lie,
Out over the top by the eagle's seat.

Watched through teary eyes, with no room for lies
As off the point they've burned.
Then reined my other half, to face my daddy's wrath
Because I hadn't got 'em turned.

Flipped hat-sized loops, and hung hidden hoops,
Where the saddlehorn can't go,
Then dallied on a stob, when I seen the cork bob,
Set back and hollered, "Whoa!"

Known the contentment of having all good equipment,
As we rode from the warming fire.
Then a lost rope and mind later, bulldogged a man-hater,
And tied him with rusty wire.

Swung down the rimrock chute, to hobble the wild cowbrute,
Where she'd jumped when she felt my line.
Then cut last strand, and heard her land,
When she crushed the stunted pine.

Texas.

Seen Dad slip 'em slack, so they'd stay off his back
In the slide off the steep granite sides;
With a fire few could fan, but a truly free man,
In a jail of tipped horns and hides.

From the hooves and heat that ruin catch-dogs' feet,
That leave red specked trails to camp,
To my mother fair, who's always been there
To pick our thorns by the kerosene lamp.

I've spent all the day's light, on stands out of sight,
With orders not to play,
To see sparks from horseshoes, then hear the news,
"I took 'em the other way."

And with cracked-lipped mumbles, between the worn-out's stumbles
Have sworn to myself right then,
That to eat and rest was but a memory at best,
And I'd never see water again.

Picked up rocks at wreck ends, to kill my only friends,
As they've weakly wagged their tails.
They'd followed since pups, through the downs and the ups,
But had lined on their last long trails.

And when the weather hot, and my thinking not,
Drug cattle on buckled knees;
Then for years had to ride by where they'd died,
With bleached skulls tied to trailside trees.

Then the flies that lit when the gutted quit,
Hooked while on the run,
Then to dig for knife, to end a good 'un's life,
Cause no real hand packs a gun.

With the forty-four years through the gore and my tears,
I've rode on this fault of land;
And the hard rocks I've rolled, and plant life I've bowled,
I claim to be a cowhand.

And since there can be little change in our cattle or range,
And it takes such a world of try;
If we have our say, and the Feds let us stay,
I'll be one when I die.

Texas.

But to be a featured operation in the *Modern Cowman* publication,
I doubt if we'd have much luck;
With hard-to-photograph herds and our unprintable words,
And boots runnin' over with muck.

Dad's now seventy-two, but his smoke's still blue,
And he hasn't begun to splinter.
We worked some tough country today, and some got away,
But they'd better bush deep this winter.

DUANE REECE, *Cowhand*
J Bar X Ranch
Winkleman, Arizona

Texas.

To me the old West was not a myth. My dad was a cowboy all his life, or a rancher, and to him, work was something you did on horseback or with a pick and shovel. He never could quite see that sitting at a typewriter or at a desk was really work. That was something you did to escape work. He tried very hard to make a cowboy out of me, but I always had two left hands. It is a good thing I had something else I could go to, but I've always sort of wished I could have done it. I still get an inferiority complex when I watch a good cowboy work.

ELMER KELTON
Livestock reporter, fiction writer
San Angelo, Texas

15

Texas.

Texas.

I always wanted to be a cowboy from the time I was a little boy. But when I was growing up I just didn't realize there really were cowboys that worked much the same as they always have. When I was living in Gainesville and going to college, I came home one day and there was a *National Geographic* sitting on the kitchen counter, and there was an article in there called "Punching Cows at the Padlock Ranch." I didn't really know what I wanted to do at the time, but I read that article and it sparked something in me. I made up my mind that as soon as that semester of school was over, I was going to go out and see the West— and see if I couldn't get a summer job on a ranch. My folks would have liked to have seen me finish school, so I didn't tell them what I really had in mind—that I had no plans to ever come back at all. When I finally landed a job in South Dakota during a branding, after the wagon came back in I wrote and told them that I liked it so well I thought I'd stay. I've had no regrets for my time being a cowboy; I've thoroughly enjoyed it. I've learned a lot of things that a feller couldn't learn in any other way—not just cowboying, but things about life. I think I've come to understand a little bit more about people in general. I've got a little different perspective on life, having lived on both sides of the fence. I came from a semi-wealthy family that comes from a long line of doctors and lawyers, and I've lived out in the cow camps on the western ranges. I've found that the people in the ranch country are not unintelligent, as some people might think. They've got a lot of common sense and a perspective on things other people wouldn't know anything about. I'm glad to have gotten to know them. My favorite kind of country is the big ranch country and my favorite kind of people are the kind that live and work in it.

MIKE CADE, *Cowboy and journalist*
Gainesville, Florida

I guess you can be brought up in the ranching business and still not like it. But I like to see good horses working and I like to see good men on them. It means a lot to me to see an old boy that can turn a cow or that knows how to work a herd and keep them quiet, or that can ride in a branding pen and snake those calves out to the fire easy. Or if a horse blows up with him, he can stay with him. I like to see cattle being driven and horses being moved, and I like to see that dust boiling up. I like to smell mesquite smoke around the chuckwagon or around the branding pen and I guess it makes me feel that I'm a part of something in this old world. I like the open air and the open country. I don't like the asphalt or the crowds. I like to see the sun come up in the morning, like to see it set in the evening, like to see the stars at night and hear the bobwhites whistle and the coyotes howl and a calf a-bawlin' for his mammy. I like to see the country in the fall of the year when it's cool and crisp, maybe right after a rain, when the smell of the land is just sort of fresh smelling and clean smelling. I like to see old cows come up when you're feeding in the winter and there's snow on the

18

Texas.

ground and you feel like you've done some good when they get their bellies full of something that warms 'em up a little. I like to see a young horse and feel like I've taught him something and feel like he's a better horse for the fact that I've been riding him. One of the main things, I like the people. Like any other business, there's good ones and bad ones. But most of them are good and down to earth, and they'll do what they say they'll do and you can bet on it.

TOM MOORHOUSE, *Rancher*
Moorhouse Ranch Company
Benjamin, Texas

Texas.

Colorado.

Here everyone is like one big family. People are concerned. It's all been mystifying to me. It's as if I've been plucked into another universe. I know I'll go back and get involved with my work and forget, but when you're out here, you think you'd like to stay.

CAROL PAFUNDI, *Nurse*
New York, New York

SPRING WORKS AT THE 06

Woosh!! It was three-thirty in the morning and Ramón, the old *cocinero*, had just doused a big pile of dry mesquite wood with gasoline and struck a match to it to start the breakfast fire. Most of the boys were still snug and warm in their bedrolls dreaming about how they were going to spend their wages on fancy headstalls and silver-mounted spurs. And then, magically, with no alarm clock, everybody would wake up and pull on their boots and put on their hats and walk to the fire. A full moon would still be hanging there, like a big silver concha in a crystal-clear Texas sky, as you poured your first cup of coffee.

"Mornin' Ramón, mornin' y'all."

"Aieeh, *comida!*" And it was flapjacks and bacon and hot chocolate, and always, just as the sun was coming up, some of the boys would be jingling the remuda, and you'd wash down your last bite of flapjack with a big swallow of hot, black range coffee, and hurry off to get your rope and claim your horse.

Those men can throw a hoolihan like Hank Aaron could hit a baseball. It would fly through the air like a bird with big wings and float down around the neck of a sorrel or a bay. Saddle up and ride out across God's country, hoping that you wouldn't look like a complete fool when it came your time to turn back a herd-quitter.

We'd trot out a'ways and the two bosses would kind of ride off to the right and to the left and split up the cowboys and take off in two different directions. You'd fall in behind the man you were supposed to go with, and just as the sun was clearing the mesquite, you'd start wondering just where in the hell all them cows were. And then the boss would say, "Gary, you drop off here, you know the way. Dave, you drop off here and work the draw and the side of the hill, and Charlie, you drop off here. Follow these tracks to the pens, and if you see any cows with two- or three-day-old calves that act like they can't make it, just leave 'em."

And you ride in a pattern like the spokes on a wagon wheel, pushing whiteface cattle and feeling like somebody just gave you the deed to the planet Earth. Breathing the dust of the working pens, and looking at the dirty, sun-ripened faces around you, you deeply realize that you are in the company of real men.

That first day, after we got the cattle penned, I was put to flanking calves and everybody pitched in to help me learn how to grab the rope and jerk 'em to the ground. Then it was dinnertime and Ramón had beans and stew and chili sauce that would burn a hole in

21

your tongue. We'd sit around in the afternoon and sharpen knives and throw ropes and talk about curb bits and hackamores and people who had come and gone.

Supper was a country boy's delight with steak and French fries and Dutch oven bread and *perro pinto,* and I never once found the coffee pot empty from early in the morning until I went to bed at night. I had never slept in a bedroll before my first night on the 06. I lay there and looked at stars I hadn't seen since I was a little boy.

One of the memories that sticks in my mind is of the morning that I got to jingle horses. It was getting rosy in the east as we rode out and split up, with heavy spurs jingling and sparks flying from the volcanic rock. Then the thunder of five hundred shod hooves stampeding to the corrals where the cowboys were lined up on foot with ropes and riatas. The hoolihans would whistle through the air as the morning mounts were led out and saddled and another perfect day would begin.

One morning at the pens they said, "Charlie, why don't you get your horse and drag a few?" Well sir, I did the best that I could and after double hockin' a calf that had already been branded, I actually managed to drag a few to the fire. I was ecstatic to say the least. One day I helped move the remuda ten miles to "the top." This was Texas at its best, standing tall and proud, high above the Big Bend country, with a necklace of horses stretched out single-file as the 06 remuda paraded up the trail, 125 strong.

Night was always a special time. We'd sit around and talk and sing and drink coffee. There's just something about a campfire. I remember one night hearing some coyote pups barking at the full moon, as I lay in my bedroll looking up at a velvet western sky, with the Big Dipper hanging so close you could almost drink out of it.

I remember Ramón telling about the days when he had cowboyed for the 06, fifty years ago, when the wagon stayed out for three months solid, when there was 19,000 head to work and they drove the steers to the railroad at Alpine. Some days later I realized that I hadn't seen a newspaper or a television set or heard a radio in quite some time, didn't know what the Russians were doing or if Walter Mondale was winning any primaries, and it slowly dawned on me how a man could "go crazy out here." I guess I went a little crazy myself because I sure did love it.

I remember watching the kids flanking calves and thinking, "Hell, there'll be cowboys, there'll always be cowboys."

And then, all of a sudden, it was over. We rolled our beds and shook hands all around, with me trying in vain to explain what the week had meant to me, but I guess you just can't put it into words. We changed planes in Dallas and we were back in the real world where people complain and sleep late.

Now I walk around with a rope in my hand, practicing my hoolihan until the spring works at the 06 come again. In my mind's eye I see evening campfires and blue Texas skies. I hear jingling spurs and the creak of saddle leather. I smell honest sweat and early morning coffee. For one short week, I was a cowboy. Damn, I was a cowboy.

CHARLIE DANIELS, *Singin' star*
Nashville, Tennessee

Texas.

Especially during tense times, my mind wanders to the morning we joined the roundup. Those images will always remain with me.

CHANA GAZIT, *Co-producer*
David Grubin Productions
New York, New York

I forget what year it was, but when they filmed *Giant,* the picture company sent somebody down here to get the lingo when we were working. You'd start talking to somebody about what was going on and they'd job one of them mikes in your face. Why, you couldn't say a durn word then!

WRIGHT HOCK, *Retired cowboy*
Renderbrook-Spade Ranch
Colorado City, Texas

Texas.

Very seldom does the weather ever bother me. I enjoy a good rainstorm just as well as sunshine. Sometimes I might say to myself, "Damn, it's cold out here," but that's the end of it. I like more or less the basic things in life, and this is about as close to basic as you can get. It puts me in the mountains, and my dad always told me the most important thing in the world was to do what you want to do. There are some hands you can have in the mountains for twenty years and they'll never be a mountain man. Then there are others who are doing an injustice to themselves and the mountains by not being there.

One day I was shoeing a horse at the Triangle X and old Jack was sitting on the porch smoking his pipe. One of the guests came up and started talking to him. After a bit the guest asked, "Jack, do you ever feel like you've kind of wasted your life?" Jack didn't say anything and the guest went on, "All you've got to show for 70 years is that old pickup." Jack just sat there and puffed on that pipe. Finally, he said, "Mister, all my life I've done for a living what you save up all year to do in two weeks." I never forgot that.

H. A. MOORE, *Outfitter*
Gardiner, Montana

You are either reaching someone—to include yourself—with your work or you aren't. Sort of like being a cowboy. You are or you aren't. You're either on the payroll or you're someone playing at it. You can have the spirit and the desire and all of that, but to me the bottom line is getting paid for it. The minute you're off the payroll, you're in another category. Which may seem a simplistic approach, and there's a lot of gray around it, but dammit, cowboys are cowboys. And I think that anyone who isn't on the payroll—and especially anyone who's *never* been on the payroll—is going to see the cowboy and move in his world differently than a genuine cowboy would. And despite a great deal of shared, common philosophies, I believe every cowboy is different. Some are leagues apart. I don't think anyone should be put on a pedestal, just as I don't think anyone should be dragged through the dirt. That cowboys are, in my opinion, at the top of the class seems to be more a reflection of what *everyone* should be, not just a certain segment of society. Cowboys are among the few people I've met that meet basic requirements for human dignity. And there are cowboys who go beyond that and are special. But I don't believe that cowboys—like myself—are without fault and can't be improved. To place *no* demands on the cowboy, not to encourage him to seek higher standards still, not to call what you believe to be a shortcoming a shortcoming, is to be blind in the worst way. As a group, I don't think there's better people than cowboys. As an outsider, I sometimes see why America is continually charmed and awed by the cowboy (most often for the wrong reasons). Most cowboys may never get rich, but at least they can say they *lived*, and that their life is worth remembering.

KURT MARKUS
Writer and photographer
Colorado Springs, Colorado

Texas.

Texas.

Nevada.

Texas.

Texas.

Romance? There's no romance up here. You should see it in December—thirty below!

BUCK ANDERSON, *Rancher*
CA Ranch
Bozeman, Montana

California.

They make all corners of the world for different people and somehow dust bothers me everywhere but here.

BUCK POUNDS, *Horse trader*
Roswell, New Mexico

I guess there was a time when people went into the cow business because there was big money in it. Maybe a few decades ago, maybe a hundred years ago, that was a good way to make a living, a good investment. So people got into the cow business to make money. Their main interest was getting the cattle worked and getting the job done, and the horse was a tool to get it done. He was expendable. You hammered on him and pried him around and sored his back and busted his feet up, cut his tongue up, jerked his head around. It didn't make no difference as long as you got your cattle worked. I think there's a lot of fellows in the business, not necessarily ranchers and owners, but just plain cowboys, that don't look at it that way anymore. I know I don't. There's nothing I enjoy more than working cattle. That's my whole life. But rather than the horse being the tool to get the cattle

Texas.

worked, to me the cattle are the means of making a good horse. The cattle are just a tool in order to help him along and make him better. I don't feel like the horse is put here to get the cattle worked. I feel like the cattle are put here to give me and the horse something to do that's just a little bit more important than all the phony stuff a horse is used for in any type of environment other than working cattle. A horse has got a pretty sorry place if he's on the racetrack or in the arena or in the show ring or on a trail ride. I'll just never believe that those horses are really enjoying what they're doing when they're in that type of place. But when he's got cattle to work, he can be a happy animal if the feller sitting on him isn't jobbing and jerking and riding him into the ground, if he's treating him like a partner and giving him a fair shake and just asking him to do a job.

JOEL NELSON, *Cowboy*
o6 Ranch
Alpine, Texas

Peple are always telling me, "Dang, you won't even be able to walk when you get older," and I tell them, "Yeah, but I'll have a whole lot more to talk about than you will."

SCOTT GILBERT, *Rodeo cowboy*
Whereabouts unknown

Texas.

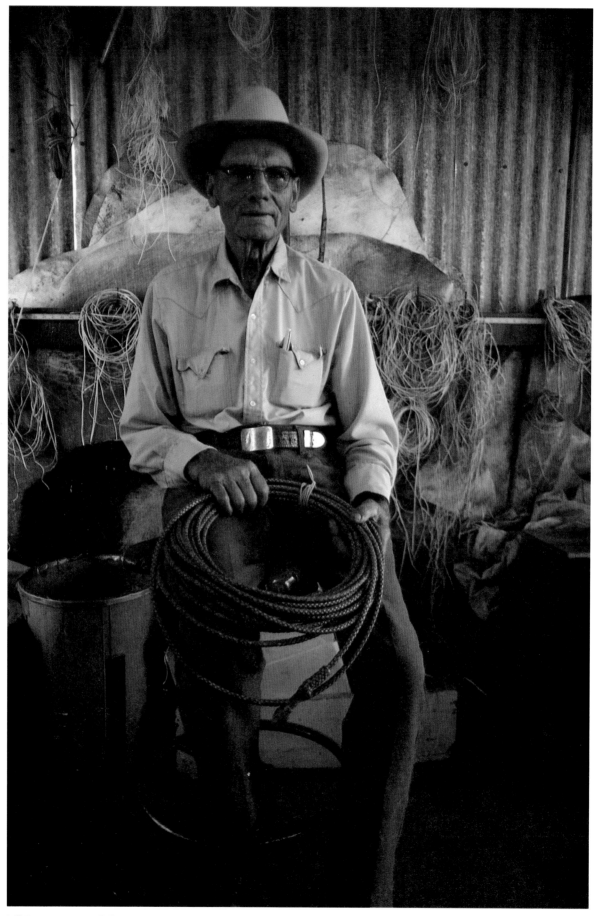

Bill Dorrance, Rawhider, Salinas, California.

CHAPTER TWO

THE HERITAGE

The old-timers and the old ways

I N CALIFORNIA I watched Tom Dorrance help a young horse trainer handle two problem horses and get them on the road to becoming useful. Tom is a little bowlegged
fellow who walks with a cane and relies on a hearing aid for conversation. The first horse
had some bad people problems and was so terrified of humans that she would try to jump out
of the pen if she was approached. She had been unloaded in a high-walled round pen where
this young trainer hung out his public shingle to help those kinds of horses. Why would a
strong, healthy, tough young man need an old man to help him handle a rank horse?

Tom approached the round pen and stood back a few feet until the mare was able to
stop running and look at him from the far side of the pen. Then he walked up to the pen
and again waited patiently until the mare stopped running and turned to look at him. Next
he hung his cane inside with her and again waited. Next he introduced a swishing plastic
flag over the edge of the pen and then another, waiting each time for the mare to stop and
accept the new booger. In only a few seconds, the young cowboy was able to ride safely into
the round pen and continue to get closer.

Tom would instruct the young man to step back and give the mare more air in front,
throw his rope only at her rear end until she could handle that. He would explain that
approaching her from the front was just too much right now, that she needed space to escape. He knew what she was thinking before she did. In an hour or so even I had my hands
on the mare, helping her get used to human touch.

The young cowboy had the skills and the physical abilities to handle the horse, but
Tom Dorrance had something else. He never set foot inside the round pen. He sat in a little
wooden chair on a golf cart just outside. Everything happened so smoothly under his guid-
ance that most people would never have believed the horse had a problem. No dust was

kicked up, no hair was knocked off, no cuss words were uttered. But a tough, a very tough horse was now standing quietly with only her skin trembling as we stroked her; soon even that was calm.

The cowboy's heritage is the old slow chuckwagons instead of the fast, expensive modern trailers; the old slow wood branding fires instead of the fast butane heaters. It's slow-rising yeast and sourdough and slow-cooking live oak coals. It's the old slow men who aren't the first to jump out there to rope a fighting bull or hang 'em in a colt when he wants to buck.

Maybe some of these outfits use a wagon and some of these old men operate the way they do for more reasons than just because they're old.

Most old men are slow and a lot of younger guys don't think they're getting anything done. But you watch them old men and they'll get more cows worked easier and never get out of a trot. Them young guys will be dashing over here and dashing over there and they're running by a lot of opportunities to get the job done smoother. But an old man, he knows that if he gets too fast, he's going to get out of control. So he won't go fast. He'll stay slow and wait for the opportunities to come. These young guys, they think if they ain't kicking up a lot of dust, they ain't getting anything done. When they're doing that, they're in a wreck 99 per cent of the time. There's a lot of old men that's just as reckless as anybody else, but usually them old men, they've been in enough of them wrecks that they're slowed down. They know what doesn't work. Maybe they don't know always what *does* work, but you can see some stuff that they do. They get themselves in a situation that you might handle one way and they'll handle it a different way. Maybe they'll handle it that way because they tried every other way and they got in a wreck.

MARTIN BLACK, 26, *Buckaroo*
Gamble Ranch
Montello, Nevada

Our father would take me out when I was five or six years old and get old gentle cutting horses and put me on them. He'd have me hugging them around the neck trying to stay on. In fact, they used to turn from under me. I've got so stiff and stove up I can hardly get on a horse anymore, but I can still get on. I like it. I always said these folks who are out jogging and one thing and another, if I wanted to get exercise, I'd rather just take a nice cutting horse and get out and cut out fifteen or twenty steers. That's what I'd rather do.

Grady Nelson, Meriwether Ranch, Alpine, Texas.

I wouldn't say I was any expert but Jack Pate's a mighty good one. As far as saying who's the best, that would be hard to say. But Jack would line up with them. Of course now he's too old to do what a lot of these younger ones can, but knowin' what to do and when— why you couldn't beat him.

WATT R. MATTHEWS, 86, *Rancher*
Matthews Ranch, Albany, Texas

Before we ever lay a hand on a horse, we teach them to line up. We preferably run them in a small, crowding alley where they can't run around a whole lot. Then if they give you the behind, poke them until they turn around. You can do it with a plastic pipe, a whip or anything. Here we use a sotol stalk. You have to have lots of patience. If you have a horse or two that already know how to line up, it helps to put them in there. But sometimes we

35

just work colts from scratch. Last year we weaned some colts one day, and by noon the next day they were lining up. From then on it's just a matter of habit.

They used to line up mules by teams in Muzquiz to pull wagons. The first man I ever heard of to do it with horses was Bill Finan, who ranches west of Muzquiz. He started back in the early forties. One of his cowboys, Felix Vasquez, came to work for my father as his foreman during the forties and we started doing it too. Vasquez later went to the U.S. to work at the Chaparosa Ranch in South Texas. After seeing how they caught their horses by running them around the pen and roping them, he asked if he could teach them to line up. He said he knew an easier way to catch horses.

There have been some years when the mountain lions just wiped me out. I have to pen the mares here every night. The Mexican government doesn't want us to kill the lions. They will send out an ecologist and biologist and you have to prove the lions are hurting you. Then, if you convince them, they will send out someone to help. By that time, you may be out of colts.

I don't like to ever have to ask the men to get off their horses. I keep a separate fencing crew. If you have anything to tell one of the cowboys, you better pull him aside and tell him when he's by himself. They have a lot of pride. They could all get better-paying jobs in town.

In the late sixties when Mexico began to eradicate the fever tick, we had to dip all the cattle every fourteen days. We weren't through working the last pasture when it was already time to start over. That led to a lot of cow work and we had to have more and better horses to stand up to it. Our area is now free of ticks but we still dip every 45 days, since the tick line is only fifteen miles south. It is a very fragile barrier. From here on north the country lends itself to gathering the cattle. South of here the country gets more rugged and brushier. The country is so rough and the cattle so wild that those people would be happy just to catch them once, to send them to market.

ALBERTO MUZQUIZ, *Rancher*
Rancho La Rosita
Muzquiz, Coahuila, Mexico

I was born in 1898 in Waxahachie, Texas, and started cowboying on the JA Ranch in 1916. Worked there two years and went to Arizona to the big Double Circle outfit on the Apache reservation. When I first went to Arizona it was frontier country. It was just like Texas was about 1890. Used to, they wouldn't let you go to town but twice a year: Christmas and the Fourth of July. Them wild cowboys would all get drunk, fight, such as that. I never did drink. I'd get away from them when they'd hit town. Good fellers who had plenty of sense would get drunk and hair-brained and didn't have a lick of sense. Kill their best friend.

Ramon Hartnett, Cook, Fort Davis, Texas.

Nicholas Bustos, 60, Piedritas, Coahuila, Mexico.

6666 Wagon, Guthrie, Texas.

All of them wore six-shooters, right on the street in town, everybody. And they could use them, too. I didn't wear one because it bumped me when I was riding in the brush and I was just a young feller and I didn't want to fool with it. I could shoot and handle one all right, but I didn't never carry one. But some of them fellers would just as soon go without their hat as their six-shooter.

And they were cowboys, I'll guarantee. That was a tough country to punch cows in, rocky and mountains and timber and brush and wild cattle. They could turn cattle just like a lobo wolf. It was wild, exciting, clean, grass country. Wasn't any weeds. 'Course you had to keep your horses shod all the time. We'd change horses every 30 days and reshoe. The others would be skint up, wore out and their shoes wore thin.

You couldn't take a big remuda with you in that kind of country—couldn't water them. That was great country, the strongest grass I ever saw. You could might-near ride a horse in the winter time on that grass without feeding him any grain. Cattle never had any diseases there, never got sick, didn't chew bones and sticks like they do in Texas. It was great cow country.

I worked for the Chiricahuas, Cross S's, too. All of them was on the Apache reservation. Biggest outfits in the Southwest. Worked for Five L's on the reservation, the Bells in New Mexico for a little while and for the Matadors in Texas. Then went back to Arizona and worked all around in that country again.

I was young, wanted to ramble back and forth. The double Circles estimated they were paying lease on 25,000 mother cows and that wasn't counting half of them. They was running them cows for two dollars and a half a head a year, and there was that many more running without paying on them. But you know, that horseshoeing finally gets to you. I wanted to ride barefooted horses a while. Also the Indians began to want to take that country back and they finally did. Took it away from them big fellers.

So I come back to the Matadors again. On the lower Matadors they used to run two wagons. Had two crews, two remudas. Quite an outfit. Probably 30 cowboys on both outfits. I remember the fall of '28, they put all the men with the lead wagon, which Claude Jeffers was running. We went to Croton, where all the wild cattle and big steers was.

We worked down in there two weeks with 36 men. We made a big drive the last day and took them north out on open country. We had a two-section holding pasture out there, and we came out with a big roundup. We got them out of the brush and cattle were coming from every direction, trying to break back and men running and turning them. Them boys knowed what to do, too! Cattle on the outside were running full-speed in a mill and them big steers was in the middle, three foot higher than the cows! That was a great sight. We got 102 big steers in that drive and some of them was sixteen years old.

We took the fence down about 50 yards wide and just eased that round-up in that holding pasture. Old Claude Jeffers had been there nearly all his life and he said that was the best drive they ever made on that country. They shipped them big old steers, rough hully things, to Oklahoma City and they brought $102 a head. That was a good price for cattle then. I believe that was the wildest drive I was ever on. We got lots of old wild crazy cows that needed to be shipped, too.

About '34, I got married and moved to the JA and been there ever since. I was thirty-five at the time and my bride was nineteen. I was a-gettin' 'em young and tender. I've got grandchildren and great-grandchildren now. I'm on the Camel Creek Camp, nine miles south of headquarters on the Red River. It's awful rough cedar brake country in the Palo Duro Canyon, but it's a good winter country for cattle. When there's lots of snow and cold on the plains, it'll be open and pleasant down in there.

The JA pulled in their wagon in '55. They had so much trouble keeping wagon cooks. The old ones wore out and the new ones didn't want to fool with these pot-rack outfits, so they pulled it in and the poor camp women had to cook for 'em.

I miss the wagon. It's a lot handier to work with the wagon, camped close to your work. I like that wagon work, still do, if I had a good cook. It's just the kind of life I like. It's free. You camp out, you can move to a fresh clean place, stake your night horse and get up the next morning and go.

Ranches, especially little ranches, are getting too modern. It's just a new class of men that's growed up and they just like that way of doin'. I don't think they've improved anything. They talk about all this technology and stuff; well, it ain't nothin' but just a big fancy word. Actually what makes a good manager is good men and plenty of good grass and water. That'll make technology for you.

Henry Switzer, at Matador, made my saddle. It's a good 'un, one of the best. He's been dead now for years and years. It's a full double-rigged stock saddle and we tie her hard and fast. I still shoe my own horses and I've got a two-year old I'm going to break. But I do a lot of work with them on the ground before I ever ride them. It might be that I can stay with him in a round corral. After I get him to handling a little, I can get by with him. But I wouldn't want to hire on just to break broncs, now, at my age.

TOM BLASINGAME, 88, *Full-time cowboy*
JA Ranch
Claude, Texas

Max Puckett, CA Ranch, Bozeman, Montana.

We quit using a wagon in the sixties. We got too modern. I kind of go for this modern stuff. I slept out around that wagon for too many years.

BILL MCCLELLAN, 60, *Cowboy*
Renderbrook-Spade Ranch
Colorado City, Texas

06 Ranch Wagon, #8 Noon Camp, Alpine, Texas.

CHARLES GOODNIGHT'S DREAM

He's been in the saddle since 'way before dawn.
He's ridin' his third horse and the sun's nearly gone.
Now from somewhere upwind he smells camp bread n' beans
And his bedroll is waitin' by Charles Goodnight's dream.

He thinks of ole timers back in earlier days
When pack strings n' greasy sacks were the most common way
Of gettin' the groceries to the roundup each day.
His bed was a blanket thrown out on the clay.

Then a rancher named Goodnight lay thinkin' it seems
'Bout cowboys n' Texas, bad weather n' beans.
So he built him a chuck box, got a wagon n' teams
Now the tents make a home around Charles Goodnight's dream.

Ol' Charlie was thinkin' when he had this idear
That a cowboy could sleep well n' carry more gear
The chuck was lots better, the cook not as mean
A rolling *cocina*, Ol' Charles Goodnight's dream.

The dream is all loaded with flour n' lard,
Canned fruit n' syrup. They's two decks of cards.
What cowboy could want more at the end of the day.
Than a bed by the dream and a dollar in pay?

Ask any good cowboy about his best times,
He'll talk of the wagon and the hoodlum behind.
He'll mention fat cattle n' grass tall n' green,
And the cavvy strung out behind Charles Goodnight's dream.

Now the wives of the wagon men pray for the day,
When the calves are all worked and their men home to stay.
They feel sorta lonesome, a little demeaned;
But they'll brag to their friends 'bout the man at the dream.

On some outfits she's been scrapped to come back again
Like a pawn on the chessboard, a victim of whim.
And she comes back far stronger each time she's redeemed.
And the buckaroos ride out with Charles Goodnight's dream.

She's a mother, a lover, a port in a storm,
The cowboy's idea of comfort and warmth
She's a home where his heart is and the coffee cup steams,
And the night horse, he grazes 'round Charles Goodnight's dream.

The harness is hung on the tongue pointed north.
The breeze rocks the range teepee poles back n' forth.
Somewhere an ol' cow bawls, all part of the scheme,
Of the life on the range, built around Charlie's dream.

One hundred-and-nineteen-plus years it has been,
And the dream has rolled out twice a year with her men.
She's been shown on canvas, in books, and on screen
But she's true to her buckaroos, Charles Goodnight's dream.

Like filings to magnets, like birds to the sky,
The dream can draw cowboys, and the smart men ask, "Why?"
But once a man's been there, it's clear as can be.
It takes strength to stay there, but lots more to leave.

She draws 'em from gutters, from off of barstools,
Some from their dad's farm, or an Ivy League school.
But whether they're rich, poor, or cultured or mean,
They're far better men when they're out with the dream.

So set up, you cowboys, and oil up your gear.
Let the drunk oil his tongue up on whiskey an' beer.
Sit tall in the saddle, your silver agleam,
Be proud you can be part of Charles Goodnight's dream.

In Nineteen-o-three, Henry Ford preconceived,
That the teams and the wagons were due a requiem
But when mud bogs the Ford down and the gasoline's gone,
Charles Goodnight's dream and her cowboys roll on.

She's been home for cowboys, a hospital too.
The cook was the doctor while cookin' his stew.
The shade n' companionship under the fly,
The brand of the outfit burned onto her side.

The old cow-buyer comes out to visit the crew.
Little fat ceegar, boots shiny n' new.
Beefsteak n' gravy n' biskits n' beans,
He buys from the outfit just to eat at the dream.

Then he watches the crew catch their afternoon mount,
For the cuttin' n' brandin' n' gettin' the count.
Whether packin' the bridle or a little too green,
Every horse has a real job at Charles Goodnight's dream.

Renderbrook-Spade Ranch, Colorado City, Texas.

44

And the ol' buyer thinks of a time way back when,
The same kinda horses, the same kinda men,
When he was lots younger and a little more lean,
And he was a cow boss a-runnin' a dream.

Some scholars say maybe the end has drawn near.
You cowboys move over, technology's here.
But somewhere out west, where the big outfits are
Out beyond highlines n' highways n' cars,
Our grandkids will work cows,
Their eyes all agleam,
At the cavvy strung out behind Charles Goodnight's dream.

JOEL NELSON, 40, *Cowboy*
06 Ranch
Alpine, Texas

My dad had two ranches. One he called the Desert Ranch, about five miles below the IL, and then the Silver Creek Ranch that was about 25 miles further up, but we called it the White Creek Ranch. My dad lost the Silver Creek Ranch to the bank during the drouth and hard winter of '31 and '32. I think for twelve months there was only an inch of rain recorded. A lot of those wild horses would paw for water and just die there. Most of the cows were smarter; they'd go find another water hole. The Double Square outfit probably had 10,000 head of horses. Horses got so cheap that they let their *caballada* go down. They couldn't handle those horses and they went wild. Those were the wild horses I knew. You could catch horses out there that weighed twelve hundred pounds, really beautiful animals. That Cow Creek was a little more inbred, and they were probably down to thousand-pound horses. But they were pretty, man they were beautiful. The wild horses in the country today started from these gentle horses getting out. I don't think there's any wild horses now like the mustangs they talk about back a hundred years. Pretty near all of those horses died in that hard winter and drouth of '31–'32. There were just a few of them left, not enough to stock the country back up. When my dad died, I had seventeen head of saddle horses and I was short of horses. I'd ride five or six horses a day sometimes. Especially when we were chasing those mustangs. That's the only way we could do it, relay them. We'd drive our saddle horses out about twelve miles and put them in a corral where we could get the mustangs in close enough. We could go up and change horses and go back and pick them up and follow them around again. If they wasn't run down, we'd go back and change horses again. If we didn't run out of daylight, we'd run them down and turn our saddle horses loose and put them together. They'd follow the saddle horses into the corrals. We'd do that in the

45

wintertime and we had a certain amount of feeding to do, so we'd get up at four o'clock in the morning and try to get that done by daylight so we could go chase those horses. The only time we'd rope something is if they gave out and couldn't follow with the rest of them. I don't know if we even took our ropes, just tie ropes. It would get so tired that we'd just get it by the tail and jerk it around until we could get it down. We'd tie a hind and a front foot together where it could get up and hobble around but couldn't get away. We had lots of horses fall down but back in those days we never did break a leg or have any broken bones. I've had lots of broken bones but that's been since. We were just lucky, I guess, because we took some awful falls. John took the worst one I've ever seen. He was running wide open and his horse picked up a badger hole. He turned end-over-end. He was hurt bad enough that he couldn't get back on his horse; his horse wasn't that gentle. My horse was gentler, so I let him ride it in and I rode his in. He was all right the next morning. In fact, the old cowboys in the old days, a horse just couldn't buck with them. I could bother one with the bridle reins enough to get by. I'd pull him around, one side and then the other, to where he never could get to bucking very hard. My dad could do the same thing with a work team. He could hook up just as mean a horse, two of them together, and I mean he could slide both of them. It was bad because he worked forty-two men and he could work those horses and they were gentle to him, but he'd give them to the other guys and they couldn't handle them.

HUGH REED, 71, *Buckaroo*
Lourence Ranch
Clover Valley, Nevada

Most of your domestic horses, what you'd call domestic horses raised around the ranch, are all used to a person ahorseback. But if you gather one of them mustangs that's ten years old, it takes him a long time to get over seeing a man horseback. I've heard old timers talk about mustangs that they've started back in the thirties and forties. They would start maybe a ten-year-old. One guy said those horses would never get used to seeing another person ahorseback, even when somebody was riding them at the time. See, a mustang out in the wild, if he sees a man ahorseback, he runs. It's his enemy. So after you start him, like if you make a gather and go to the rodear and if this horse was off alone for a long time, like say an hour or two and then another cowboy approached him on another horse, he'd throw his head up. He'd look out there and see this guy coming, the first thing he thinks about is his enemy. Even though he has a rider on him, too, he'd cut out. He was getting away, saving his life. It's hard to get them over that after they get a little age on them.

RANDY STOWELL, *Buckaroo*
Cordano Ranch
Currie, Nevada

46

Ricardo Zermeno, Charro, Guadalajara, Jalisco, Mexico.

Tom Blasingame, 88, Cowboy, JA Ranch, Claude, Texas.

Dave Ashe, Little Bear Ranch, Tres Pinos, California.

It was July, it was getting hot and there were a lot of flies. There were those yellowish ones that are real bad in high elevations, then there was a kind of gray deer fly, they call them, and I don't know how many other flies. We started about forty of those horses. We'd start early but we had to just work on through. During the day when those flies got to be at their worst, those horses would go to looking for you. I found out you could put those flies to work for you if you presented yourself to the horse in a way that he understood you were trying to help him. By using the flies, you could help hurry up that "snuggle-in" and kind of "cuddle" deal. The horse found out that you were his friend. I found out that instead of working with them when the flies weren't there, you could work with them when the flies were the worst and have help. The reaction from the flies played right into your hand. Once you get a little foundation started, then you build on it. From the beginning, we try to work from where the horse is at.

TOM DORRANCE, 73, *Horseman*
Merced, California

48

Sam Springs, Flying D Ranch, Gallatin Gateway, Montana.

Tom Dorrance, 73, Horseman, Merced, California.

I got out of the Army in 1946 and came back to Midland. I ran into Millard Eidson, the man that owned this thing, and he asked me what I was going to do. I said I didn't know, I'd just been out of the Army a week. He said, "Go to Lovington with me." And I just got in and went with him. Went to work and been here ever since. My daddy had worked for this outfit twenty years, a little bit of kinfolks, all of us named Eidson. I always did what nobody else wanted to do for thirty years. I told Millard one time I just couldn't work for a hundred dollars a month and needed a raise. He said, "I'll tell you something about these dang buttons, the more you pay them, the sorrier hand they are!" I had five daughters at the time, so I couldn't afford to quit. Nobody else would have fed us for what I could do. That's what kept me here a long time. I rode all the broncs. The other boys picked what they wanted and I got what was left. But it got to be a good job. Millard died and passed it on down to his son, Scharbauer. When Scharbauer passed away, we wound up with the whole deal, that's what the will said. It's quite a shock to just dump all this on you. Juandell and I couldn't have thrown it all away in our lifetime if we'd have just started that day. But we kind of felt the other way about it. It's no disgrace to inherit something like

49

Ted Gray, Nicasio Ramirez, Otis Coggins, Gray Ranch, Alpine, Texas.

this, but it's a danged disgrace not to do something with it. Make it better, take care of the people that work for you. It's the biggest, flattest place on the face of the earth. There's no better cow country in the world than right here if you could just get twelve inches of rain. But lots of times it only rains six. The bad years sure outnumber the good, or they have in the thirty-eight years I've been here. But it's just like any other ranch country: if it wasn't drouthy or rough, there'd be something else here. They'd be farming it or something. You can ride out on these baldies and see for five miles. It's different, but I like it, I shore do.

BOB EIDSON, *Rancher*
Cross HE Ranch
Lovington, New Mexico

We just started from scratch. I never had to serve on a jury because I wasn't a land-owner or a householder until '41. My daddy went broke during the drouth of '17 and '18 and had to sell the ranch. I moved my brother away from there in 1920, and it was my ambition to go back. My niece tells a story that one day I went down to milk and turned the calf in to suck and stood there daydreaming about owning that ranch. I forgot to take the calf off and he got all the milk. I just dreamed of owning that ranch someday. Always, that was my ambition to buy it back and we did.

TOGO MOORHOUSE, *Rancher*
Moorhouse Ranch
Benjamin, Texas

My father's name was J. H. "Long John" Burson. He homesteaded some land that is presently in the JA Ranch. One time we went up to look at some bulls on the WHR— Wyoming Hereford Ranch—and Daddy really embarrassed me. He said, "Those little old sawed-off things are not worth a hoot. The calves won't be big and how many men you got here, anyway? I've already counted about twelve or fifteen! And how many cows?" They said, "Well, we run four hundred cows." He said, "Hell, me and a Meskin ran eleven hundred cows and branded a thousand and fifty-three calves one year, by ourselves. I don't think we got any use for your cattle."

JOHNNY BURSON, *Rancher*
Double Diamond Ranch
Silverton, Texas

I started cooking for the W. T. Waggoner Estate when I was thirteen. My daddy was the wagon boss and the cook got drunk and they fired him. Daddy just came in and told me I was going to cook. I've been cooking for the Burnett Ranches' Four Sixes since 1968. If you ever get started doing this, they just won't ever let you quit. Cooks are notorious for bad tempers and notorious for being drunks, so when they find somebody who just *threatens* to kill but acts pretty good, then they keep you in the same job.

We used to change maybe fifteen times in the two months the wagon was out, but now we pretty well stay in one spot. The Sixes is so big, if it happened to rain where they were camped, they'd have to quit work. This way, if it rains on the north side, they go work on the south side, or east or west. But I believe I liked it better when we changed camp. We had the mules then, hood wagons and everything. It was harder work but I liked it better. Just romance of the West, I guess.

I usually have a coal-oil can that sits over by the woodpile and in the mornings I use coal oil to throw on the wood to build my fire with. I'd run out, and I asked one of the cowboys to get me some more coal oil. I guess he wasn't paying any attention, because he brought me gasoline instead and he didn't tell me. The next morning I bent down with my head in the stove there, threw that gasoline in there and, man, it went everywhere! There was a kid right there sleeping and I slung gasoline across his bed, burned up his bedroll and nearly caught the tent on fire. I was just expecting coal oil and it doesn't do anything. When I threw that big can of gasoline in there, by God, everything liked to have went at once, I guarantee you.

JOE PROPPS, *Wagon cook*
6666 Ranch
Guthrie, Texas

My granddaddy brought the first two black men ever into this country, Slick and Jerry. Slick was cook and of course they put him horseback too, but ol' Jerry was a bronc-ridin' dude! My granddad sent him after the horses one morning before daylight. Old Jerry jumped him a lobo wolf, he thought, and was just going to ride up and rope him. It was before daylight and he couldn't see very good. He roped that dude and it was a panther. That sucker squalled and liked to have scared old Jerry to death. My granddad said he came back by the barn dragging that panther, screaming, "Kill him, Mr. Nick, kill him!" But he was already dead. He'd drug him plumb to death. Granddaddy said he saw a horse buck with Jerry one day and buck into a tree and broke his leg right above the knee. That leg was just flopping but that cowboy never did quit riding. Said he was a tough son-of-a-gun.

BOB BEAL, *Rancher*
Beal Ranch
Gail, Texas

Antonio Gutierrez, Rancho La Rosita, Muzquiz, Coahuila, Mexico.

Broke lots of horses, oooha! Broke three every year for Jesse Merrill for twenty-one years. Broke horses for the Leoncita Ranch when I was sixteen. Broke ribs seven times, broke knee, broke ankle, broke both wrists, broke shoulder. So I said, "No more!" and I quit.

RAMÓN HARTNETT, *Camp cook*
Ft. Davis, Texas

The less you know about me, the better off you are.

BRYANT EDWARDS, *Cowman*
Edwards Ranch
Henrietta, Texas

Mountain Island Ranch, Glade Park, Colorado.

I just hate to see my old cows go. I don't have anyone working for me, just hire some extra help when I need it. I haven't been replacing cattle very fast and they've all gotten old all of a sudden here. A lot of these registered breeders, they don't actually have much contact with their cattle. They have a herdsman and a manager and so forth. But where you're just kind of raised with them over the years, it's hard to do. They are sort of like old friends. I think an awful lot of all of them, and yet to raise good cattle I don't think a person should get married to them. You leave things in there that you shouldn't. You won't get rid of a cow because you *like* her and yet she doesn't do the job that she really ought to do. A person should view them as a business and leave the personality out of it. It's just sentimentality, kind of like an old horse. You just finally turn them out to pasture and say, "Well if you have a calf, fine. If you don't, fine. Go on and die here somewhere." They're not really worth a whole lot when you sell them on those conditions anyway.

OWEN WOMACK, *Rancher*
Menard, Texas

54

ill Zimmerman, Cross HE Ranch, Lovington, New Mexico.   *Duck Valley Indian Reservation, Owyhee, Nevada.*

In 1955 I and another boy named Bubba Christian worked at the Horsethief Canyon camp. We were very young and inexperienced at the time, but it made a lasting impression on us, and we certainly gained valuable experience for future endeavors. How they ever put up with us I will never know, but I'm sure glad they did. It's sad to see so many of the good ways of life change, and to think that many of the things you are now experiencing, as those who came before you did, shall never happen again.

AL BROTHERS, *Manager*
H. B. Zachry Co. Ranches
Laredo, Texas

Hawkeye Sanford was cookin' for John Scott. Hawkeye was about seventy-five years old then. He was probably ugly when he was a baby, but he was really ugly when he was seventy-five. Dick Songer was there and he'd just recently got married. Dick came in the cook tent one morning and had breakfast. When he got up and threw his plate in the wreck

55

pan, he said "Hawkeye, you sure are a good cook, but my new cook is a whole lot better lookin' than you are." Old Hawkeye just said, "Well, give me a chance to fix myself up a little!"

RON GODDARD, *Cowboy*
Penokee, Kansas

Somewhere along the line, my dad bought for a dollar a head a whole bunch of these big Cleveland Bays and blooded horses. They weren't saddle horses, they were mostly for those fast stage coaches. But he crossed them on the mustangs since mustangs were smaller. My dad had about twenty-five hundred head of these horses in the twenties and the bottom fell out of the horse business. There they were, running on the range, thousands of them. Everybody ran their horses together on the desert, and we had big spring roundups and everybody parted his horses out. They'd run them in corrals and catch this colt on this mother and brand it and turn them back out. We'd catch them and ride them just for fun, but most of the time my dad took them to the railroad unless there was something in there he wanted or somebody else wanted. Very few of them we kept, most of them just went to chicken feed or dog food or something. That's what I did in my early twenties was run these horses.

After '24 and '25 we started these big drives, taking them to Red House, Golconda, and some went to Winnemucca. We sold thousands of horses. The Double Square ran a lot of horses and they were going broke and nobody was catching their horses. So my dad took the contract to catch them. We got seven or eight dollars a head for them. Big market, huh?

One time we had about two thousand head of horses at Juniper Basin when we were gathering all these horses and shipping them out. They made us kids herd them in the daytime and then they'd put them in the corral at night. This particular night was a nice moonlight night. Along about one o'clock in the morning we heard, "Get up! Get up! The horses are getting out of the corral!" I was one of the lucky ones that had a wrangle horse up. I was sure sleepy. But these old-timers made you wake up. By the time I got up there, about half of these two thousand horses had already gotten out of the corral. They were going up a draw and this dust would boil up and just lay there. All you had to do was ride up the side of it. You couldn't see nothing in that dust. Didn't know if there were horses in there or not. That was the most beautiful thing I imagine ever seeing. Them horses going up that draw, the dust rising, moonlight. It was about five miles long, that many horses running. When we got up to that rimrock, that string of dust was eight miles long. I don't think I've ever seen anything like it since.

Mountain Island Ranch, Glade Park, Colorado.

Obra "Uncle Arb" Denton, Pecos, Texas.

Everybody liked horses. In those days, transportation was all done with horses. Now you go down there to that Owyhee desert and you can go anyplace in a darned automobile. But when I was a kid you didn't. We'd go from one place to another with our pack horses and our beds and our *caballada* and there was no roads. You just took off across country. There was no fences, nothing there. You made your own fire, you packed your own groceries. Nowadays you go over here with a truck and trailer, and when you get there you got everything under the sun to eat or drink. In those days we didn't have nothing.

JOHN J. REED, 75, *Buckaroo*
Willow Creek Ranch
Jiggs, Nevada

CHAPTER THREE

COWBOY

*How they look to the world and how
they look at it*

D URING THE PAST FEW YEARS there has been quite a controversy about what to call a cowboy. In the high deserts of Nevada, Oregon, and Idaho, he's called a buckaroo; in California and Mexico, a vaquero; in South Texas, a brush hand; and the styles go on and on. I give these titles with some hesitation, since a title that is complimentary on one ranch might be an insult even just across the fence. The differences stem from styles of gear and how the cowboys do their job, but as they've traveled around the country, sometimes these styles begin to blend. I've seen chink-leggin'd Texans dally on slick horns and Oregon buckaroos in shotguns ride double-rigged saddles. Seventy-one-year-old Hugh Reed, an Elko County native and well-respected old mustanger said, "Buckaroo or cowboy, I don't think there's any difference. One might call someone a buckaroo and another would call him a cowboy and there might be a difference but I wouldn't know." On the same subject Cotton Elliott, a Texas cowboy who can make a hand in any kind of country, said "When you go to turn a cow, there's only one right way to go turn her. A good buckaroo turns one the same way a good cowboy does. His equipment's different but his style is the same as far as handling cattle."

The cowboys in this book are here because I think they should be. I've only scratched the surface but these are the best I've met. Some, of course, might be farther along on mastering the skills or the dress code, but to me the best cowboys go beyond that, as you can probably read between the lines of this book. The cowboys pictured here are my friends, although they may not all claim me. These are the people I accept collect phone calls from. These are the people who can pull in without notice and demand a hot meal, a dry bed, fifty dollars, and a fresh horse. If I've got it—it's theirs. I'm married to one of them and I still hope my daughter grows up to marry one too.

Bill Dugan, Nye, Montana.

But they're not perfect, yet. At least one of them has an alter ego that drinks too much, fights and wrecks things. A few are so bad we had to change their names to keep their whereabouts a mystery to the good lawmen on their tails. One, however, assured me it was fine to use his name because every time he'd gotten in trouble with the law, he'd used an alias. His favorite alias, he said, had always been "Barney Nelson."

One late night in Nevada I switched on my tape recorder to interview an eight-foot Owyhee Indian who wore a black hat big enough to park a pickup under. "What's your name?" was my first nervous question. "Barney Nelson," he answered and folded his arms across his chest.

Having cowboys for friends is a test of endurance.

If I only went to town once or twice a year that would be enough for me. Most of the time, when I get my paycheck, I mail it to the bank while some of the other guys would go in to the casinos to cash their checks and have a good time drinking and gambling and come home hung over and broke a couple days later. Maybe I missed something somewhere, but that never looked like a good time to me. I like to go to Jordan Valley to the rodeo and to the Elko County Fair. I can see a lot of my old friends and neighbors there and find out the local news for the past year. A few places I've worked had telephones but most of the time we were in a camp that didn't. We would go to town about every four or six weeks to get groceries and buy a pick-up load at a time. It might seem lonely to someone that was raised around a lot of people, but I was raised this way.

The place I'm at right now is a little over a million acres and they run about seven thousand head. I get up on one of them mountains and just about everything you can see belongs to the ranch, depending on where you're at. You get on one side of it and you can look to the other side and you can't hardly see any of the country of the neighbors. It's about fifty-five miles from one end to the other, any direction you want to go. It's a pretty quiet life.

I know there's some of these young guys who go down here to Capriola's and they buy a big hat and a pair of suspenders and they think that's all there is to it. Once they get a job on one of these big outfits, they think that's as far as they need to go—and that's as far as a some of them do go. They never try to improve their horsemanship or their cowmanship or anything. Some of them think the bigger wreck they get in, the more western they are. But that's just the opposite with me. The smoother you can get it done and the quicker you can get it done, that's how I measure a cowboy. Somebody that's out of control most of the time, as far as I'm concerned, they need to look for a different occupation. But to each their own. Who am I to judge?

These cowboys, who, like I said, go down and buy a big hat and a pair of suspenders, they look at them Will James books and them Charlie Russell books. Well, ninety-nine per

61

cent of them Charlie Russell pictures, they're in a wreck and they think that's what it's all about. I guess they never worked around anybody who could get the job done smooth and easy and quiet. A lot of these big outfits, the owners aren't there to keep a handle on that. But anybody who was raised handling their own cattle, you just don't *do* that. Anytime you get rough and tumble, you start knocking the calves out of them pregnant cows and that's your profit. But some of these young cowboys, they never see it. They never see the pounds they're knocking off the cattle or the calves that the cows abort from jamming them and roping them. I like to rope as much as anybody, I'd say, but there's a time and a place for it. You don't just go out and start roping these old cows and choking them and putting chewing tobacco in their eyes just for the fun of it. To me, that ain't what it's all about. That just shows that they can't do it any other way. Most of them can't even get the job done that way. If they'd take a little more time, they can get that cow to working for them and they can get a lot more done if they'd just sit back and watch. A cow is one of the dumbest animals there are, but if the cowboy can't handle them—well, what's that say for the cowboy? Horses are a little different. Horses are smart, smarter than most cowboys. That's why a lot of these cowboys aren't riding any better horses because they can't figure the horse out. But, hell, you take a cow, she's one of the dumbest animals there is and you'd be amazed at how many cowboys can't outsmart a cow.

MARTIN BLACK, *Buckaroo*
Gamble Ranch
Montello, Nevada

I always wanted to work for a big ranch and the Sixes was always my idol of a ranch. I knew the men and the wagon camped within five or six miles of us in two or three different places. I used to go up there when I was a kid on weekends, stay Friday and Saturday night. That's where I always wanted to work on a big ranch. After I got out of high school, the wagon boss, Bigun Bradley, and George Humphries, the manager, came by here visiting. I wanted to go, bad. I had already talked to Daddy about it and he wasn't much for it. He always had plenty to do here. None of the other boys had ever worked out, we'd neighbor but we always worked here. I didn't think he was going to let me but he said, "If you want to work up there for a while, it'll be all right." So I asked Bigun and he hired me. I was just seventeen.

I can look back and I think I'd 'a made a mistake if I hadn't worked off somewhere. I think it's good to work around different places when you're young. But then when you get older, I think that needs to cease. You need to stablilize and get somewhere and get with the program and stay. My daddy was a cowboy but he was also a ranch man, and if there was fences to build or hay to haul or farming to farm or roads to build or ditches to dig, well, that's what we did. I look back and see guys that all they were willing to do was sit on a

Ron Goddard, Penokee, Kansas.

Tom Moorhouse, Moorhouse Ranch Company, Benjamin, Texas; Mike Stephens, Moorhouse Ranch Company, Gail, Texas.

horse, and they're limited. The more knowledge you have of all of it, whether you're doing it yourself or overseeing it or hiring it done, the more efficient and better job it'll be. So I don't regret anything I've ever done. It's not belittling to me to say that I've done a little of everything, and as far as that goes—I still do.

We spend the biggest part of our time horseback, but when something needs doing, we get down and do it in a second. That's how I feel about anybody that works for us, too. I respect a cowboy's wanting to be on a horse because I know how he thinks, and that's where he's going to stay most of the time. But when it comes to doing something else, if he doesn't want to do it, then he needs to go somewhere else other than here. When we hire a cowboy, needless to say we like experience. But their willingness and their attitude are far more important than any other thing. For instance an experienced man with a bad attitude will do you more harm than an inexperienced man with a good attitude who's willing to learn. Also we want people who think positive and who are optimists. For their benefit and ours. If they're negative and pessimistic, they're not going to do themselves or us any good.

As far as the top cowboys or the region they come from—the guys that come from the open country have to adjust to working in the brush country. The guys that go from the brush country to the open country can handle it. But it's just adding another factor that has to be dealt with. Most of the guys in this country savvy the brush, so most of the guys we hire are from around in this area.

TOM MOORHOUSE, *Rancher and cowboy*
Moorhouse Ranch Company
Benjamin, Texas

I was just born to it I guess. My kids are fifth generation, so I guess we inherited the lifestyle. I guess it's something I've always wanted to do and had no desire to do anything else. It's the cows that put us there and the cows that are keeping us there. Cows and horses go hand in hand. You can't have one without the other in our business.

My wife and my kids, I can't do anything without them. They've saved me from being late for supper lots of times. We hire a couple guys—the kind of guys that can do anything and do it quick and quiet and no bones about it. They have to be able to do everything from packing a shovel to fixing fence and feeding hay. He has to do everything I do. When a guy knows the difference between a cowboy and a cowman, he's usually a pretty good man anywhere. He can weld, he can do anything. He's got a good head and that's the better man. The best horsemen I know, they can weld, irrigate, fix fence with anybody and they're still the best horsemen. A guy learns more about stock when he's doing a little bit of other things, like fixing fence that a cow tore down. It makes him think a little bit about what that cow was thinking. Or if a horse tears his saddle up, then while he's fixing it, he gets to thinking about why that horse tore it up.

I've never been hurt by a horse or a cow—just my feelings, lots of times. If you want to do it without a lot of fuss, there's a way you can do it most of the time if you stop and think about it. If you get too rough with stock, you got to pay for it later. If you make your living on them, you're just defeating yourself.

JOHN DELONG, *Rancher/Buckaroo*
Trout Creek Ranch
Winnemucca, Nevada

THE COWBOY

The term "cowboy" brings to the mind of the average tenderfoot a rather rough character arrayed in a pair of leggin's, a broad-brimmed hat, boots and spurs, and a big red bandana handkerchief around his neck—a character that is not especially fitted for any vocation, except that of a movie actor.

In spite of these false impressions, the fact is evident that it requires more skill and efficiency to qualify as a modern, up-to-date cowboy than for any other occupation in the known world. The cowboy is familiar with the nature and instinct of livestock. He knows how to handle and care for the herd—how to round up, cut and separate cattle; knows how to circle and quiet a stampeded herd. He can discern between excellence of quality and breeding and the inferiority of the scrub. By observation, he knows when range cattle are on the mend or decline. He knows how to brand: just where the brand should be placed, how it should be made, and how deep to burn to avoid blotching. He knows how to select old cows and culls that should be marketed. He knows that a bronco horse should be given slack when his forefeet leave the ground, and should be ridden with a hackamore until he learns the rein. His qualifications and attainments are innumerable.

Besides being an expert in handling horses and cattle, he must be a blacksmith, competent to shoe horses, shape running irons, and do general repair work. He is necessarily a butcher, and can slaughter a calf and cut it into steaks and roasts. He is a cobbler, and can half-sole boots, and mend saddles and harness. He is a carpenter, and can saw to a line and drive a nail straight. He is a botanist, and is familiar with the nutritious grasses and weeds that fatten, and also knows the poisonous plants. He is a mechanical engineer, and is competent to repair automobiles, mowing machines, hay balers, windmills and pumps. He is a cook, and knows enough to boil beans until the bacon can be cut with a spoon. He is a doctor and a surgeon, and can treat a case of bots or colic in horses, or cure a case of screw worms or bloat in cattle; is also familiar with the effects of calomel, salts, castor oil, liniments and pills.

He is a lightning fast calculator—how else could he dodge the limbs of mesquite and catclaw, as he plunges his horse at breakneck speed through jungles and underbrush similar

Ty Holland, JD Ranch, Kent, Texas.

Shot Branham, 06 Ranch, Alpine, Texas.

to those of southern Texas? He is an athlete, and when forced to run a race with an enraged cow to see which can reach the fence first, he always does his best.

Nothing is more amusing than to watch a tenderfoot trying to pass as a cowboy. His first impulse is to don the accustomed attire; but when he's asked to bust a bronco, bulldog a calf, or shoe a horse, the fun begins.

The cowboy must have not only skill and efficiency, but endurance. He works twelve hours more often than eight, and sometimes eighteen, as the occasion demands. Quite frequently he is compelled to miss his noonday meal. His duty demands that he face all kinds of weather. Rain, hail, sleet, or snow does not cause him to falter, but like the Good Shepherd, he responds to duty.

Take Roosevelt's regiment of Rough Riders, made up as it was of cowboys hardened to the work on the range, accustomed to self-denial and all kinds of hardships—it is no wonder that they forged to the front and made a world-famous record by their endurance, loyalty and bravery.

LUCAS C. BRITE, *Rancher and cowboy*
Brite Ranch
Marfa, Texas

First published in *The Producer,* magazine of the American National Cattleman's Association, April, 1929, when Mr. Brite was president of the association.

I don't know how you'd define a good cowboy or a bad one. It depends on the country you work in. You see guys that might be from flat country—they might not be as good a hand in the mountains as guys from this area, but we might not be as good there either, or in the brush as fellers that live there. Your methods will vary with the type of country that you work in. I know I'm surely not the best—or the worst. I guess I've never done anything outstanding, but I've done a little bit of everything. I'm in the middle somewhere I guess, just average.

BIT ROBERTSON, *Cowboy*
Alpine, Texas

I like to work for a bigger place where they kind of do things the way they used to instead of doing it all out of a pickup. A lot of country, if you can get to it, that's the way they do it, but if you can go to rougher country, you got to use horses then. My next request would be an absentee owner. Where a man would leave you alone and kind of let you do what you think is right and if you're not doing it the way it ought to be done, he can get somebody else. I don't feel like you need a nurse-maid around all the time. If somebody has to be around to tell a man what has to be done every day, he wouldn't be much help to anybody. I like a boss who is not afraid to do what he asked you to do. I don't like to see one hollering and screaming all the time. If he's got control over his men, he doesn't have to say too much. The men respect him.

It's kind of a rat race in town. They got to be at work at eight o'clock and then they get off at noon and they got thirty minutes for dinner and they get back and they get off at five. Here, you haven't got any set time. You eat when you get there, and when you get through you go back to work. It's not on a schedule. It kind of falls into place on its own.

You learn something new every day. I don't think any one man knows it all. You can kind of tell what kind of hand a man is just by looking at his equipment. If he doesn't have any decent equipment, you can tell right then that he doesn't have any pride in what he does. If that's the way you make your living, you need to have some good equipment. It's just like any other business: welder, mechanic or anything. If he doesn't have the tools, he can't do it. Some of them take it a little more to heart than others in trying to look the part or play the part. They like to wear the clothes and the spurs in the beer joint, but that's about as far as it goes with a lot of them. Pride, I think it's good, although if a man's gonna look that punchy, he needs to be a pretty good hand. If not, it might turn out pretty bad for him.

TY HOLLAND, *Cowboy*
JD Ranch
Kent, Texas

clockwise:

Raymond Jayo, Oreana, Idaho.

Randy Stowell, Cordano Ranch, Currie, Nevada.

Dave Corlew, Lebanon, Tennessee.

69

GOD'S FUNNY CREATURES

I was ridin' my ole cow horse 'cross the prairie flat one day,
When a little voice inside of me piped up and had her say.
She said, "Ya know, Dakota Territory would be a right fine place to be,
If all our dang ole cowboys were give to Tennessee!"

I shook my head and smiled, with a grin a mile wide,
And a little feather tickled me, all up and down inside.
I said, "No need to worry, it ain't really all that bad,
There's cowgirls clear across this land had days just like we've had."

In a gentle little whisper, I said to me, "Hey self,
We've got to live here with these men, we can't put them on a shelf."
So self we must remember, that they're a breed all of their own,
It's either bred right in 'em, or it's the way that they've been grown."

They're a different kind of creature put here on God's good earth,
We maybe have a rib of man, but they've inflated worth!
They think that they are 'macho,' and a notch above us gals,
But they too have their failings, and we really should be pals.

Just cuz they can't remember the day that we were wed,
But know which cow had which calf, five years ago, instead.
And maybe they don't notice when we have a brand new look,
But we know their eyes are workin' when they read 'her' like a book.

When things at home need fixin', there'll be something else to do,
Like help a neighbor more in need, or on the fat just chew.
They'll pull dead calves and wade in slop, it's an awfully dirty chore.
But changing messy diapers makes 'em gag, they now implore.

Then, of course, they're helpless when it's time to find their socks.
They're in the drawer in plain ole sight, I guess their eyes are rocks.
Their fashion sense is weary, they think checks and plaids will do.
We tell 'em that the shirt is green, and they'll argue that it's blue.

They holler when the grocery bill seems too big in months gone by,
But there's dollars in their pocket for drinks when ace is high.
They never understand our moods, and our crying seems so silly.
They beg to know what's eatin' us, then wow—think it's a dilly.

Their bachin' days are over, we've done spoiled 'em, don't know why.
And when *he* has to cook for *him*, he throws the grease on high.
They leave a trail behind them, be it mud or clothes or dirt.
They simply can't imagine how these things could really hurt.

Waddie Mitchell, Stake Ranch, Jiggs, Nevada.

They say they're strong and virile, believe it if you can.
But when they get a cold or flu, they're more like Peter Pan.
A curlew in the grass now moves and makes my cow horse shy,
So we forget our macho men, me, myself and I.

JO CASTEEL, *Rancher and cowgirl*
TC Outfit
Vale, South Dakota

Cotton Elliott, Alpine, Texas.

I rode into a typical West Texas team roping one day with my horse in a double-rein rig. I was packing a sixty-five-foot rope with a rawhide honda and had my leggin's and wild rag on—definitely anything but team roping attire. I asked Sid to rope with me but he wouldn't even speak. I went ahead and got some partners—somebody that didn't know me—and was catching all right and doing a fair job of dallying. There was a fellow sitting there next to Sid and he said, "Gol-lee, watch that old kid dally!" Sid wouldn't talk, so this fellow came over there and asked me where I was from. I told him, "Up North." He said he figured I was. Well, the next steer I came out on, I roped him good enough but I missed my dallies and dropped about sixty feet of rope on the horn and made a big bird's nest. Sid was laughing and said to that old boy, "Yeah, look at him dally now." That fellow was getting a little skeptical. He came over there and asked me just how far up North I was from. I said, "Oh, about fifty miles up here at Salt Flat."

I've always enjoyed being a little different, I guess, and making people laugh—letting them know it's not all that serious. I'm proud to know there are people like Rocky Reagan, James Kenny, Bill Evans, Tom Blasingame, Ray Hunt, Bill Dorrance and Charles Marion

72

Russell who are enthusiastic about the way of life they chose and are willing to share their thoughts in order to encourage others to lead their own lives. I feel that enthusiasm and good attitude got more horses trained and cows penned than experience and pessimism ever did.

I don't like barbed wire, grease, or rubber, but cowboying ain't dead and as many good hands are being made as ever. I think as long as we continue to harvest grass with bovine balers, there will be good hands riding good horses even though the message may vary with years and country.

I knew cowboying was what I wanted to do even though I had a lot of discouragement at a younger age from my parents, teachers, and the people you look up to. Everybody tried to talk me out of it. The people I came in contact with didn't have a background in it and didn't consider it a reputable occupation. I think a man with enough desire can do anything he wants to do. I don't think it's a matter so much of talent as it is hard work. I got burnt out with some aspects. I was spending too much time doing things that I didn't enjoy doing, that I thought were unnecessary.

I bought this horse Diamond because he had a horrible reputation. I've always felt real close to a horse that had a lot of problems, I guess because I've always had some myself. He's torn up a few things—torn up a round pen, broke a few nylon ropes—but he's never bucked me off. I don't think things that come easy are that good.

MIKE CAPRON, *Cowboy*
Fort Davis, Texas

Let's see, how'd that go? This fella left his horse tied to the fence and went to dinner. When he come back out, he hadn't noticed it all morning, but he had his saddle turned around. He'd been lookin' off the south end all morning! He got to thinking, I guess, that since he'd made that little batter, he'd do something to somebody else and make them think they couldn't remember what they was doing either. So he took this other poor innocent soul's saddle and put it on the tail of the windmill. It was easy to see but hard to find up there. Joel Nelson was who saddled his horse backwards and then he took my saddle and put it on the tail of the windmill. Fall of '71, I believe, at the o6.

But it was kind of a diversion, you know. Somebody getting tied to their bed, or—there was an outhouse up at Nine. Somebody went in there and somebody else roped it and shut the door on them so they couldn't get out. I don't remember who was in there, but I think I remember who tied the door shut. Yeah, Stephens, I think was his name. Oh, we'd work the cattle when we could get around to it.

I got on a horse up there at Nine one morning and I hadn't rode him but a few times but he never had pitched. We were just leaving. The remuda was already pulling out. They were going right out in front of the gate and he started like he was gonna run. I reached up to get a hold of him and he blowed up. About the second jump, I hit in front of the saddle. Next jump I was on the ground and he was coming right over the top of me. I run into the gate post trying to crawl out of his way—skint my head up. He bucked up through the middle of the remuda and run them off. Took 'em about two miles to get ahead and get them stopped. In the meantime, this horse shucked my bridle and tore it up. I had to get something else and put on his head. So I got all fixed and got him back in the pen. Got on him and hung 'em in him and all he did was crow hop. So I didn't get much back and it cost us about 30 minutes getting started.

Another time, same dadgum horse, I'd rode him all morning. I'd been through the Big X-Bar and was coming up the road, going back to the house and my rope string broke. This horse's name was Mike. John Roberts named him after me. My rope string broke and it went trickling down his shoulder. I just reached to grab it and when I leaned over, I knew I'd done the wrong thing. He made a jump towards the pavement and then he whirled back. I got behind the saddle and the next thing, I went off his back end. He run off pitching. I was just walking down the bar ditch. A fellow pulled up and he was driving along beside me. I finally looked up and said, "Well, there's a loose horse down there." He said, "Yeah, and he shore didn't like you, did he?" And then he just drove off!

MIKE STEPHENS, Cowboy
Moorhouse Ranch Company
Gail, Texas

My brother was sick. He had the flu I guess. Anyway, we rode down across there about twelve miles and there was a bootlegger that made this moonshine whiskey. So John says, "I think I'll go see if I can talk him out of a bottle of that whiskey. I think it might be good for my cold." I thought it might be too. So we went up there and got a bottle of whiskey. Then we went about another twelve or fourteen miles further. It was getting awful hot and we kind of went up on this little rise and got off our horses. I was going to take the saddles off, they were awful sweaty. I had these hair bridle reins and my horse threw his nose down to scratch and stuck a front foot through there and then just started spinning like a top. I couldn't hang on to him. He got away from me and just took off like a streak of lightning. John said, "Oh, God, I don't feel like catching him. Take my horse and go." So I got on his horse and I went about two or three miles before I could catch him. This was about ten o'clock in the morning.

Well, John went to sleep in that sagebrush. I couldn't remember where I'd left him and I couldn't see him. I tried to pick up the tracks but there were range horses out there all over and lots of fresh tracks. About four o'clock that afternoon, he got up. He was only about three hundred yards from me. I knew he'd went to sleep but there were rattlesnakes crawl-

Mike Thomas, Owyhee, Nevada.

ing around and I killed three or four of them while I was monkeying around there trying to find him. Anyway, when he got up, I thought I'd get a drink of that whiskey. I thought it would be something wet anyway. But he'd drank it *all!* It was late and we went to this old camp over there. We were dry, thirsty as can be. We dipped up some beautiful bluish water, just ice cold out of the well but it was just full of rats. John drank it anyway and finally, I took my handkerchief out and strained some of that water and drank it too.

HUGH REED, *Buckaroo*
Lourence Ranch
Clover Valley, Nevada

I've learned more out here doing what I'm doing than I would have in school in fifty years.

CHRIS LACY, *Rancher and cowboy*
o6 Ranch
Alpine, Texas

Joel Nelson, 06 Ranch, Alpine, Texas.

Jeff Gray, South Dakota.

Me and Pete Smith and Lee Jones and Charlie Blue was riding across Frenchie's Meadow and we're all nice fellows—but maybe not all *that* nice. We'd been hazing around the land of plenty that summer and spending all our proceeds in town in dens of iniquity. That's what we'd *been* doing. This is what we were doin' right then: we were riding across this meadow and seen these wild strawberries and went to eatin' on them. It was kind of a stormy day. We'd been down there grazin' for quite a while and there was a big bolt of lightning hit in some timber not too far away from us and a loud clash of thunder. Pete Smith, he looks up and around at the skies and says, "Boys, we better scatter. If I was the Lord, I don't think I could pass up an opportunity like this!"

It is early spring here, cool, wet and the trees just leafing out. Bedded down under clear, starry skies last night but had to leap up and seek shelter in a smelly old barn. Had a skunk walk over me sometime in the night. I tried to lay real quiet and think nothing but kind thoughts about skunks (and keep the tarp over my head). He wandered off after a while, so I guess it worked.

RON GODDARD, *Cowboy*
Penokee, Kansas

Once in a period of three months, I was in the hospital five times. And it's not that I'm sloppy or careless, but this is ranching country. These old ranchers, they're cowboys. If they got a horse that is half-decent, they'll keep it and break it themselves. But if they got one that's hurt somebody or messed up, and you hang your shingle out, they're gonna bring it to you. I break about seventy colts a year and I've only sent one animal home, and that was a mule. It was one of those deals where the fellow said, "Aw, he's gentle as a dead pig, you won't have any trouble." So I wrote a little poem about that:

> Gentle as a dead pig,
> Was what the man said.
> But I got on to ride him,
> And the pig wasn't dead!

NYLE HENDERSON, *Horsebreaker*
Hotchkiss, Colorado

I think it was the summer of '76 that I worked at the X Ranch in the Panhandle that lies south of Dalhart and west of Channing. The headquarters of the Long X at Dalhart is one of the old XIT division headquarters. It was a good summer job. I was prowling and riding through the cattle in the morning and then in the afternoon we'd take care of whatever we'd found that needed attention.

Along in August, we were gathering bulls. Just north of the headquarters is a five-section pasture where they kept their heifers. They were running black Angus cows at the time and they would put Longhorn bulls on their heifers. There were ten bulls in Five Section, as it was called, and we spent one day gathering them. We had a little trouble with a couple of them and managed to get eight. Tom Black, the foreman, was going to be gone all the next day so he told me that I might go out to Five Section and try and gather those other two bulls. I saddled up this little nine-hundred-pound Texas cow pony that I had in my string and went out to try and get them.

I knew they were going to be some trouble, so when I found the bulls I threw them in with some of the heifers and tried to bring them in together. As I was nearing the pens, these bulls kept lighting out on me and I couldn't keep them with the heifers at all. So I tried to just bring them in together. That didn't work either. So I just had to go one-on-one with them. I finally got one bull through a gate that goes into the horse trap, after a lot of hard riding, and I had one more to get. I found him and started him toward the horse pasture too.

As you go down that draw toward the horse trap, there's a windmill about a hundred yards from the gate. I'd get that bull lined out towards the gate, and as we got near the

78

windmill he'd turn back on me and I couldn't hold him. We made several pretty wild sashays through the salt cedars. I had no success in ever getting him past the windmill. About the third or fourth time around the Five Section, we started playing cat and mouse around the windmill. In that country, most windmills empty directly into a big aluminum water trough. The bull got on one side of that aluminum tub and I was on the other side. I'd start around that tub, try to break him away from it and head him towards the gate and he'd run around the tub. He kept the tub between himself and me. We were going back and forth around that tub, he'd feint one way and I'd feint the other. I was somewhat irate after being raked through the salt cedars, so I did what I ordinarily would not have done. I took my rope down and tied it hard on my saddle horn. I was planning to get him lined out toward the gate and as soon as he turned back, I was going to stick it on him.

Well, I finally lined him out away from the trough and we made a big circle around there. My pony was kind of tired and I was having a hard time getting in position to rope this bull. Just as we got to the trough, I threw a heel loop and I was just going to try to double-hock him and maybe somehow tail him down. I'm not sure how I was going to do *that*. Anyway, I threw this heel loop just as he jumped into the trough. I caught both hocks but my rope pulled up on only one. He was standing right in the middle of that water trough and turned around and started hooking at me. I tried everything to try to get him out of that water trough. I tried to booger him out. I tried to drag him out. But I couldn't get him out. So I sat there a while and pondered the situation.

I had two long braided nylon piggin' strings made out of parachute cord on my saddle. They were pretty long strings. I took them and built a hondo in the end of one of them and tied them together. That bull was just standing there facing me, so I got off my horse, built me a big old loop and wallered it around both of his horns and pulled it up tight and tied him to one of the legs of the windmill. I took the rope off my saddle horn and left him there in the drinking tub, tied to the windmill.

I went to another camp, told the fellow my situation and asked him if he'd come help me get this bull loaded in a trailer so I could haul him to the bull trap. When we got there the bull had gotten out of the tub and was standing there tied to the windmill with my piggin' strings. This other fellow was the son of a world champion steer roper and I don't know what he thought, but he didn't say much. Anyway, we both unloaded our horses. By that time my rope had come off his hind foot and I got my rope and we both put ropes on him and drug him into the trailer. We got the other bull penned and loaded them both on a trailer and hauled them up to the bull trap several miles away.

It's kind of a sand country, and the sand blows a lot and you often times have to dig out the cattle guards so cattle won't just walk across them when they fill up. The bull trap cattleguard had filled up and we hadn't gotten around to cleaning it out yet. So when we unloaded the bulls in this trap, we stretched a rope with a bunch of tin cans tied to it across the cattle guard to keep those bulls in there. Well, there was this old man that was sure enough a cowboy in his day, but he was old and crippled up and couldn't see very well. He'd been off doing something that morning and came back through the bull trap and didn't

Bob Blackwell, Melville, Montana.

know those bulls were in there. When he came across that cattle guard, he didn't string the cans back up. When the boss came driving back in late that afternoon, there were ten bulls standing in the road in the Five Section with the heifers. You couldn't find a better guy to work for than Tom Black, but he *did* wonder what I'd been doing all day.

MIKE CADE, *Cowboy*
Gainesville, Florida

I've been cowboying off and on about thirty years. I'm sixty-three now. I've worked all over Arizona, New Mexico, Oregon and Texas. I guess about one of the wildest wrecks I ever had was on an old fallin'-over-backards horse about 1940. I took about thirty minutes to get him saddled up, my cinch pulled up where I thought I could ride him. I was going to lead a bronc and had him tied up under a tree. I thought I had this old horse uncocked and rode him around there up under this tree, jerked the slip knot and started to lead the bronc off when that old horse set back. When he did, I just took a couple of turns on the horn with my lead line and that old horse started to fall over backards with me.

Well, I released my dallies and kicked my feet out of the stirrups and at the same time put my rein hand on top of his head. That horse came back down and jumped off about a four-foot bank with me. Thank God I had on some long gooseneck spurs and they just kind of went in between the old horse's belly and flank cinch and hooked. Kept me from going off over his head. He hit out in the middle of a creek, water about knee deep, and was just a-buckin' right there in that creek.

I was hanging out over his head with my spurs hung under the flank cinch on both sides and I just grabbed him around the neck, got a good mane holt and kind of choked him down. My body had him kind of blindfolded so he finally quit bucking. I slid back down his neck and got in the saddle and stepped off on a big rock there. I rolled me a cigarette and thanked God that'n was over with.

OBRA DENTON, *Cowboy*
General Delivery, USA

We only get time to ride broncs about once a week. Don't want to teach them too much at once. We had a humorous day here a while back. One afternoon I caught this colt, Sober Sides, and he is inclined to buck. Sometimes he is just pretty handy about it, so I hobble my stirrups for about an hour on him. He had been turned out for three months so he knew what rest was. When I stepped on, he was a little gentleman for about fifty feet and

Jess Brackenbury, Tres Pinos, California.

then did he hump up! He went to bucking right toward a young cowboy I've got who's just starting, August Larson. He was putting a snaffle bit on his horse when I said, "You better have that horse untied from the fence." August looked up and his eyes came a foot out of his head. He said to heck with his horse and jumped on the top rail of the fence. That scared his horse, Alpo, and he fell back. Since Augie had his McCarty stuffed in his pants, it hung up and Alpo pulled him off the fence into his front legs. August sure looked funny between Alpo's legs and Alpo even stepped on his hand. Well, Sober Sides didn't want any part of that commotion. I hit the back side of the corral and was coming back by, still on a bucking horse. I said, "Why did you jump on the fence? This horse is *gentle.*" I can usually visit with people when I got my stirrups tied.

Dean Tobias and I started a bunch of colts on the IL, thirteen head. Some of them were Dean's personal horses. He had three that were just dirty trash, kick you in the belly, tough. Dean's a good friend of mine, so I was helping him out riding this one at five dollars a ride. I got hurt on the sixteenth ride. I don't think Casey Tibbs could have rode him that day. He twisted my spine and slipped my pelvis. I didn't get paid for that day because I didn't ride him back to camp, I ended up getting to ride in a pickup.

Mike Capron, Fort Davis, Texas.

Nyle Henderson, Hotchkiss, Colorado.

Gary Morton, Lincoln, New Mexico.

I finally got my twenty rides in and got my hundred-dollar bill. But I decided to help Dean out and ride this horse for nothing, for experience. It's a challenge, you know, to ride them kind of horses. This horse was really tough. Dean had two more and they were just as bad. Well, the next time I rode him it was raining a little bit. Dean and I kinda overslept that morning, didn't get breakfast. We just had time to catch a horse. We were going to pull a circle so I called for "Snowball" and Dean took this "Whiskey."

I had to rope Snowball's front feet to hobble him and just as I got both feet picked up, he took off. We use a long rope in this country and I had about a seventy-foot rope, so I was going to set him down. I set down on the rope and slipped on the grass and down I went and away went my horse.

I finally got him back over there and just did have him hobbled when Dean hobbled old Whiskey with a thirty-foot catch rope. Well, here comes old Whiskey runnin' away and he runs right under Snowball's neck. Here comes Dean on the end of that thirty-foot rope. Dean went down but I was able to stay on my feet somehow. Well, there goes Dean out across that old wet grassy meadow on his belly, but he hung onto that rope. Old Whiskey finally got tired of dragging two hundred pounds with his front feet and stopped. We got our saddles kind of jockeyed around and got them up close to them horses again and got them

84

Clay Bartran, Tres Pinos, California.

Burl Hollar, Lewis Ranches, Clarendon, Texas.

saddled up. The boss, he kept looking back at us. He's getting awfully impatient. He'd waited thirty minutes on us already. And I was kind of upset because I didn't have any coffee. Pretty soon the boss hits a long trot and the next thing I know I'm running neck to neck with him and I can't stop. The boss is outrunning me and we're really flying down through the country then! Of all places, he cut me off on a circle up on a mountain. We could go pretty good uphill, but every time I'd turn around and try to come off—ho–ly smokes! Down off of there we'd come, pretty rapid.

That was one of the last times I rode that horse. Dean sold him to the YP Ranch for six hundred dollars and I got two hundred from it. Got a hundred for riding him and Dean gave me a hundred-dollar bonus when he sold him. But I didn't make any money. The company paid for the chiropractor but I paid for the gas and motel rooms. I was chasing a girl at the time, so I'd come in the night before. I was three hundred dollars in the hole on that ride.

I'm still single, over the hill: thirty. Blackie is what a lot of people call me. I've worked on Ellison's Spanish Ranch, Squaw Valley Ranch—they were really good outfits. That IL Ranch, I worked there. Worked on a couple in Oregon, the MC and the Roaring Springs, which is part of Diamond A of Arizona. Been on a few more, quit a lot of them and go right back. They always treat you better when you go back, you know. I wouldn't go very far,

85

Chris Lacy, 06 Ranch, Alpine, Texas.

might just go across the fence, go ride another string of horses. I really don't know why, I think it's the spirit. I liked the challenge of different horses. I'm starting to like horses that will turn around now, but there for a while, I just craved a jumping horse. Course I was on the ground a lot, too.

BILL BLACK, *Buckaroo*
MC Ranch
Adel, Oregon

I was on the IL wagon at Tuscarora and Dean Tobias was there. We needed some meat in camp, so the boss, he says, "When we gather today, we'll just pick out a nice fat yearling and butcher it." So we gathered and branded a little bunch of calves there and we picked out a yearling to butcher. I necked this yearling heifer and then Tobias heeled her. One of the other fellows working there, Harold, he jumped off his horse and was going to cut her throat. Tobias had his pistol and he said, "Harold, get out of the way. I'll shoot her. Harold, get out of the way. Harold, get out of the way." Well, Harold had his knee over this heifer's neck. He was going to cut her throat and he wasn't paying much attention to Tobias. So Dean shot one shot up into the air and said, "Harold, did I hit her? Where'd I hit her?" Harold was sitting right on top of her head and was looking all over trying to figure out were this bullet had gone. So then Tobias says, "Harold, get out of the way." And Harold got out of the way that time.

I pretty well stayed right around Elko. Sometimes I'd go home and help Dad a lot, too, whenever he needed help. I was just happy here. Loved the country, liked the people. I just didn't want to go anywhere else. I did work on some different outfits around, but I never did get out of northern Nevada much.

One time I was running our brood mare bunch that we got in quite often and this saddle horse I was riding fell with me. He kind of went end-over-end about three times. I was under him on the first roll and he broke my collar bone. I got up and run and tried to catch my saddle horse but I couldn't get ahead of him. That was the first thing on my mind, to catch my horse. After I could see that I couldn't get ahead of him, I could feel that my shoulder wasn't right. So I reached in my coat and felt my collar bone. I could see it was broke. So I started walking and just fell in behind the horses. They were on a trail that was going to the ranch. I followed them on home about three miles. Just before I got to the ranch, I finally caught my saddle horse. But when I got on him, I couldn't stand to ride. He was kind of nervous, wanting to be with the other horses and he'd jig along there. That was just too much movement for my collar bone, so I had to get off and lead him. I went home and put a sling on it and I had to go a hundred and eighty miles to get to a hospital. But a collar bone isn't that bad a break.

RANDY STOWELL, *Buckaroo*
Cordano Ranch
Currie, Nevada

I ride a wore-out, double-rigged Franklin-made saddle. It's flower stamped, or at least it was. Some parts are stamped, some parts just aren't there any more. It's swell-forked with bulldog taps for the brush. It has a four-inch cantle, about a sixteen-inch seat, and a horn on it I can dally or tie hard and fast. I do both, but I tie hard and fast most of the time. It depends on what I'm riding or what kind of country I'm in. If I'm riding a horse that's not very good, I tie so I know I'm gonna have whatever I rope. I've got him or he's got me.

On colts, I like to use a hackamore. I have some good ones, but I get just as good results with an old piece of rope as I do with a rawhide bosal. I grew up using them and it doesn't bother my image one bit.

I wear shotguns—real heavy ones. Most of the country I've worked in has real heavy brush. If it's not just too thick, I like working in the brush and rough country. It's a lot more reins and romals. I wouldn't use them in the brush, because they'd hang on the brush too much. If one snags a limb real solid, you can't just let it slip by and get a hold of it again. I think they're real nice lookin' and a good piece of equipment if you know how to use them. It's hard to keep a good light-mouthed horse working rough country. They're continually getting a rein hung on a limb. It takes the fine edge off a horse that normally would be light and you end up having horses that handle pretty heavy. But it can't be helped. There's no way around it and they'll handle well enough to get the job done.

I'm real choosy about where I work. I usually know them by reputation. Sometimes I know them personally, but usually just by reputation, visiting with other cowboys. I enjoy working cattle and I enjoy riding horses. I like working with a large crew of men; I don't particularly enjoy working by myself. I think lots of ranchers have over-modernized and their horses and cattle have suffered from it. Their cattle don't handle properly and their horses certainly don't.

I'd sell a bunch of pickups and horse trailers and helicopters. In the last six or seven years, there've been a few ranches start *de*modernizing. I think they've got their heart in the right place. I don't condemn all modern ways of handling livestock. I think all of them are good in the right situation, but I think too many people expect too much from modern techniques. They depend on a pickup and trailer to get their cow work done.

COTTON ELLIOTT, *Cowboy*
Alpine, Texas

I've been into Nevada, Idaho and Montana. I've worked for Simplot in Idaho and Montana and the IL Ranch out of Elko, the IM Ranch, Matador Cattle Company, and I worked for Stadtlers. Now I've been day-working for about a year. I like it a little better. You're more independent. You don't get the same monotony, the same people around every day. You get to see more country, more cattle, and you don't blow up as often at the same boss. You just work five or six days or two weeks and you go to a different job. You make more money day-working, if you work steady. But you got to kind of listen to them. You can't make your own circle.

Really what I'd like to do is lease a ranch and run my own steers, pasture cattle and be more independent. Some people are probably just content to work for the same outfit for twenty years and others probably want to do the same thing I want.

CLAY BARTRAN, *Cowboy*
Tres Pinos, California

88

Rene Duykaerts, Charlie Liesen, Jordan Valley, Oregon.

See, all the rest of these reservations, they got a lot of mines and they go to work in the mines or the highway or something. Around here, all there is is just cows. Either you be a cowboy or you be a drunk or a bookkeeper and type eighty words a minute. Big deal! There's nothing else to do. I don't feel any sense of prejudice. If a man's a cowboy, he's a cowboy. If he's a buckaroo, he's a buckaroo. It don't matter to me whether he's a white man or Indian or black or anything, as long as a man knows cows, knows horses and does his job. I've run across one or two guys who say, "Hey, Indian, hey." I just play along with them. Them guys that are always wanting to say Indian or nigger or Polack or whatever, they're the worst hands that I ever saw. I'd say they feel that way because they're a little insecure about themselves.

But I ain't really run across a lot of people that would say something like that. I'm proud of my heritage and kind of embarassed too because I ain't took more part in powwows and stuff. They never taught us to take part in stuff like that. When I started kindergarten, the teacher we had, she always told us, "White kids are smarter. White kids can do this. White kids can do that. They're smarter than you Indian kids." And the trouble was, she

89

clockwise:

Randy Glover, U Up and U Down Ranch,
Fort Davis, Texas.
Tommy Vaughn, Leoncita Ranch, Alpine, Texas.
Brian Larremore, Marathon, Texas.

was Indian! She went to a Bureau of Indian Affairs school, the same school my dad went to. That's why I never learned to talk Paiute or Shoshone. Dad knows both them languages, but I could never get him to teach me. It had been beat into his head, "Don't teach your kids to talk Paiute or Shoshone and don't teach your kids them traditions." Maybe somebody in Washington thought that if Indians can't learn their own native language, they'd abolish Indians.

But it don't work. You turn us loose out in the brush and there's always going to be one Indian that knows the native language. He's going to know the name of this hill here, that hill there, the morning songs, evening songs, the horses, the water. He's going to sit there and he's going to teach everybody. But I never was fortunate enough to learn that shit, so here I am sitting out here trying to earn my living as a buckaroo.

MIKE THOMAS, *Buckaroo*
Owyhee, Nevada

On a big outfit that changes hands a lot, if they've got some good horses in their cavvy, them horses are exceptional individuals. They've had umpteen jillion riders on them and nobody ever took the time to really do anything with them except ride them. If he can take the stress of having so many riders on him in a year and still make a good horse, he's exceptional. You run into just as good of horses in one state as the next state's got, and then again some that are just as bad. There are mediocre horses everywhere.

Sometimes you run into horses that somebody will be calling a bridle horse and it's really a grazer-bit horse. In the Northwest, if them horses never pan out and never handle good enough, they won't put them in a bridle. A bridle horse should be a handling fool. They should be able to turn around, side-pass, do anything you have to do on them. Some of the snaffle-bit horses might be a lot better than others. Some of them are just old circle horses that all you do is go out and make a gather on and others are all-around horses.

I've led circle on a few places where I'd been there long enough to know my way around. But I'd rather let somebody else do the bossing so I can cuss them instead of them cussing me. I think a boss should be a good hand and know what he's doing and have been around enough that he's come across most situations he's gonna come up against. He doesn't have to be the best friend of everybody on the crew, but he should be fair to everybody.

I'd say Harold Smith, we called him 'Smitty', was probably the best cowboy I've ever been around. He's confident in his ability and can watch you make a mistake and just laugh about it and go put the pieces back together, regather the herd, whatever. He doesn't get upset. He can get along with any kind of horse; he knows cows. He likes to teach younger guys who are willing to learn. He knows several different styles of cowboying.

I've quit every job I've ever had. One time the cow boss quit and we all liked him, so the whole crew just rolled her up and left—just out of courtesy to him. It doesn't take much of a reason for me to quit. I just get tired of one place after a while. I think a guy can get to where he'll quit *too* easy and that's bad, but as far as moving around, I don't see anything wrong with that.

Whenever you start thinking you know everything, you quit learning. When you get to that one certain point where you think you know it all, you stay there the rest of your life. As far as punching cows, you could punch cows for a hundred years and still wouldn't know it all. There's something new every day.

A good cowboy is somebody who can go to any man's country, do it his way, and make him a hand. I like to work where they very seldom, if ever, ask you to get off your horse. They don't have to pay that much. Nine times out of ten, if you've got a straight riding job, you probably won't get paid very well. I like good country to ride in, and some good horses to ride. It's the only way I know of making a living where it doesn't seem like you're working. There have been a lot of times when I'd sit back and think, I'm going to have to grow up someday and get a real job.

JEFF GRAY, *Cowboy*
South Dakota

Here comes a twenty-three-year-old kid that's been an actual buckaroo now for a year and a half. I mean he's been drawin' wages and has worked on twelve different outfits in that year and a half and he's just a top-notch hand. By God, he comes out and tells you that if he can't do it horseback, he ain't gonna do it! That pretty well tips you off. The fellows who will tell you that are generally not worth a durn horseback either.

A good hand is good any place you put him. It don't matter if you're digging a ditch or greasin' a tractor or writin' a letter. It might not all turn out just as good as he wants it to, but he's puttin' all he's got into it. You gotta be willin' and you gotta be awake and you gotta do what needs to be done at the time.

They get it from the magazine articles. They get it from the Will James books and the other young cowboys sitting around talkin'. And they get it from the old guys who never made it even to a boss's job on an outfit. He's never took on a bit of responsibility and has bummed around the country all his life. They really look up to him. He's thirty-three years old now and he's really been around. He don't want to get off his horse and he's also the guy who's going to quit you if the work gets tough. Anybody that's been around these ranches very long knows there's lots of work to 'em and it's not all horseback. These guys that're too good to get off their horses, to me it just tells me something about 'em.

WADDIE MITCHELL, *Buckaroo*
Stake Ranch
Jiggs, Nevada

92

Bill Evans, X Ranch, Kent, Texas.

Three of us were out riding some young horses and just decided to take the dogs with us. The dogs jumped a lion up there pretty close to the house and put him up on a big bluff in some rocks. We sat there and tried to figure whether we could kill him with rocks or not. We were afraid he'd hurt the dogs—so I just pitched a rope on him. Another boy got a rope on him and we drug him off that rock. I sent the other boy back to the house after the pickup. We had a dog cage there and he loaded it up, and with the two of us holding the lion between us we got him down to the road, got him in the cage and hauled him to the house. It was probably a two-year-old female, seventy-five or eighty pounds.

That Adobe Walls Ranch is big open country. It's sixty-five miles south of Alpine and those cattle are pretty wild. We rope lots of wild cows. They're Brahman crossbred cows, and they get away a few times and you got to go in there and rope them and get them out. When there's just two or three of you, somebody's got to do it. I've done it quite a while and a lot of them boys that go with me, they hadn't done it that much. They think it's pretty wild but really it's not. I didn't realize I had a reputation as being that good a cowboy. I guess I must talk a lot.

APACHE ADAMS, *Cowboy*
Alpine, Texas

This black eye? I was shoeing a horse, pulling the nails up, and caught the hammer. But I don't tell nobody that. I tell them Mother hit me. This scar on my nose? I cut my whole face off from the forehead down, teeth out. Horse blowed up and bucked under a lean-to tin roof. It improved me quite a lot. I used to be terrible ugly. I had a lot of plastic surgery done and it made a big difference. Mother was happy and the kids didn't know me.

I like to work with my family. Gosh, for fifteen years we worked that way. My wife and kids did everything along with me. I'm kind of a firm believer in a man doing everything— anything that needs doing, you do. Mother and the kids and I we ride, work, do any damn thing needing done. But I don't like to work that hard anymore. In all reality, I'm a lazy son-of-a-gun and there's a lot of things I don't like to do no more. So you see, there's no gain without some loss and vice versa. I guess you get tired of being where you're at.

Places change. I don't change. I don't like change, so if a place changes, I just leave. But the country is getting so small, there's no place left to go. You got no room. You got to go someplace where it's either too rough or too dry and nobody else can make a living either. I guess that's why we've moved around. I doubt if I'll ever grow up, you see, so I don't have any plans. I don't *make* plans. I take one day as it comes.

I went to work because I needed a job. Worked in South Dakota, Idaho, Wyoming, Nevada and lots of places in between. After you've worked for enough of them crusty old son-of-a-guns, you either get that way or you go the other way. It's not hard to keep men if you just leave them alone and look at things from their side, off and on. Everybody can do *something* good. Dwell on the good parts. To hell with what they can't do good. You can fill in that hole somewhere else. Treat them just like you'd like to be treated yourself.

I've had a bunch of good fellows. That's been my good fortune. I haven't done a damn thing for them, but they have for me. There's good people everywhere if you give them a chance. It's kind of too bad, a fellow gets older and he realizes he hasn't done much for his family, living this way. But you do what you can and the worst thing you can do is regret it. That's no good for you or nobody else. A cowboy's family hasn't got nothin'. Oh, they had a good time, but they ain't got nothin' else. They've done lots of things nobody else has ever done. They'd probably say they wouldn't trade it, but I wouldn't trust 'em. They're kiddin'. Yeah, they're kiddin'. You realize you probably should have done something else to maybe do your family better, but by that time you're so crippled up you can't pass a physical for a good job. So you're stuck. Buckarooin' for a living just beats working. And I'd hate to go to work.

ROYCE HANSON, *Cowboss*
JD Ranch
Carlin, Nevada

Wally Wines, Livingston, Montana.

Sam Dove, JD Ranch, Kent, Texas.

Ray Hunt, Mountain Home, Idaho.

Martin Black, Gamble Ranch, Montello, Nevada.

Bill Black, MC Ranch, Adel, Oregon.

I got here in Montana about the first of April and started working for Les Best. I was feeding with a team and calving-out heifers. I was there two months and went to work for Padlock's on the wagon. I day-worked here on Padlock's and Crane Ranch at St. Xavier, Montana, till the end of July. Then went to Jackson Hole, Wyoming, for a month and wrangled dudes, packed horses and such for a month. I came back here to Hardin a few days ago and am going to be here at least through the fall. If I'm here steady through the winter, I'll either be here or Connolly Division at Crow Agency or the south end at Ranchester, Wyoming. I really do enjoy it here. This is really a good outfit. Hope I can stand the winter if I'm here. We start processing and weaning yearlings next Monday. We're supposed to do over twelve thousand head in twenty-nine days. Gonna be pretty busy, I guess.

CLAY LINDLEY, *Cowboy*
Padlock Ranch
Big Horn, Montana

I believe that a good cowboy doesn't necessarily have to be a good horseman. He is tough. He knows a cow like it was part of his family. He can go all day in the desert without a drink of water, stay horseback all day with just some beans and a tortilla in the morning. He is a hell of a tracker. I judge him on how he handles cattle, not how he handles the horse. It's hard to find a good horseman who is a good cowboy. We have a lot of poor people in Mexico, but the cowboys are the only ones who are proud of what they are.

CARLOS OCHOA, *Vaquero*
Chihuahua, Mexico

I guess I like it. I just grew up into it, I guess. It's about the only thing I ever wanted to do. I've had all the opportunity in the world. I could have gone to college and graduated and got me a job. I can do anything I want to, I just don't *want* to do anything else. I had a real job once. I quit the Sixes my first year in high school when that minimum wage was two dollars an hour and I was getting that big government money at a good paying job, working for the county. I was janitor at the courthouse there at Guthrie, dang sure was, about two months. I could get a lot easier job, fool around, drive around and do nothing, sit around coffee shops. It would be all right for a while, but I couldn't do it very long. I would be bored to death. I'll keep on, probably, until I get too old. Nothing else interests me.

DONNIE SLOVER, *Cowboy*
Paducah, Texas

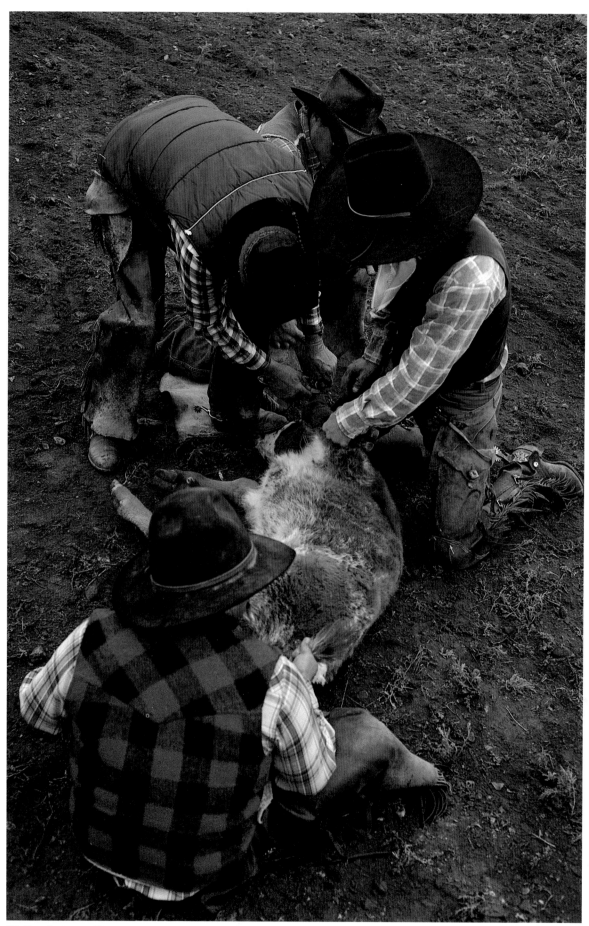

JD Ranch, Kent, Texas.

CHAPTER FOUR

THE WORK

The only real definition that makes a cowboy a cowboy

MY LITERARY HERO, Elmer Kelton, once told me that his tough rancher father thought work was "something you did on horseback or with a pick and shovel." Elmer said his father "never could quite see that sitting at a typewriter or at a desk was really work. That was something you did to *escape* work."

On the other hand, Ray Hunt, the best hand with a horse I've ever seen, has a different outlook. He was raised working horses on a three-hundred-acre Idaho farm and dreamed of someday having the chance to be a buckaroo. When his opportunity was on the horizon, he immediately came down with diarrhea. Nothing seemed to help and he kept it for several months until his first day on the TS wagon in Nevada. "I didn't think I was going to be much good," says Ray. "I thought I'd be off in the bushes with my pants down. I didn't think I was troubled about it but the day I went to work I got over the diarrhea. It left just as quick as it came. So I got to ride them horses and chase them cows and rope the calves and brand them. I couldn't believe that you could get paid to do that kind of work." The other good hands working there with Ray would try to dampen his enthusiasm with comments like, "Just wait until the work starts." "But," grins Ray, "it just never did."

This chapter is on the cowboy's work, if you care to call it that. It is this work that makes a cowboy a cowboy—not his dress code. It is the work and how well he performs it, not his ability to rope or ride bucking horses or his outlook on life. As in any profession, there are those who get by and live for Saturday night and payday, but there are also a few who never stop striving for a better way to handle a herd or communicate with their horses. Their coffee pots boil long before daylight as they anxiously await another day. They may forget about dinner or never notice that it has started to snow.

Those are the kind I like to photograph, and although our days often stretch to fourteen hours, for them and me, the work has never started.

Cross HE Ranch, Lovington, New Mexico.

Lots of times you get up real early and stay out real late, and if somebody was asking my advice I'd say, if you don't like it, don't do it. It's not just a nine-to-five job. It's something that you live with day in and day out. There's not a set time to get off. It's just something that you better enjoy before you tackle it. It's not a job, so to speak, it's a way of life.

BIT ROBERTSON, *Cowboy*
Alpine, Texas

It's our Latin nature. We work for a living but we don't live to work. Mexican time is very elastic, we take life easy. We don't have the efficiency that other people have. We have a different perspective on life.

CARLOS OCHOA, *Vaquero*
Chihuahua, Mexico

100

U Up and U Down Ranch, Fort Davis, Texas.

I think you have to start at the feet. If a horse doesn't have feet, he's not going anywhere. A lot of show people don't pay any mind to a horse's feet. They can find a horseshoer to fix that. But we ride our horses here. They've got to be sound. We took our two stud horses to the track, hurried them, and they never took a crippled step. They never missed a race or missed a day by being lame. They were sound then and they're sound today.

Another thing people have gotten away from that we try to cultivate is travel. You get on any of these geldings and go off across country and it's pretty easy, pretty nice. These little short cutting horses just eat you up if you've got to go anywhere. We don't go for any high-trotting, rattle-your-teeth kind you can't keep your saddle on.

But something I think people have cut too hard on is disposition. You get these horses too gentle, too nice and they get like everything else. They haven't got any *want to* left in them. I know one outfit that had a lot of trouble getting their horses broke, so they went to hunting a stud with disposition. They worked on it and worked on it until it got to where they'd lope off two or three miles from the ranch and they were afoot. A kid could ride any one of them, but they couldn't go anywhere either.

That's one thing about these Go Man Go horses, and these Flashy Go horses of ours.

101

The first thing you got to do is get them gentle. Every one of them will pitch if you let them. If one ever throws somebody off, watch out, because you've got something going. They get a little smarter every day. But if you get them gentle, they're just danged pets. It's more in the way they're started than in how they're bred. You can't do it without this good help.

I think—big, little or any kind of ranching operation—anybody appreciates a good horse and likes to have one that they can say can do this a little better than anybody else's horse. Like we are, raising our own horses, it kind of behooves us to let these boys do something on them instead of saying, "Tie your horses and we'll do this afoot." It kind of fits everybody better. And you can do it a little easier horseback if you do it right. Of course that's something else that's kind of got to be a lost art in a lot of places. When you just don't do it, directly the cowboys don't know what they're doing. We gather our cattle, throw them together, cut out the dry cows, anything we got to ship, cut our bulls out and run them off, pen our cows, strip cows off and drag our calves up and brand them and turn them back out—all with horses.

I think every cowpuncher likes to ride a good horse and this is how you get a good horse, not on the ground walking around a-slammin' gates. You got to do something on them outside.

BOB EIDSON, *Rancher and cowboy*
Cross HE Ranch
Lovington, New Mexico

Around here ranches usually get together to brand. They have a barbecue after and that's their pay for helping each other. They don't hire much day help to brand. There's a couple places I work that will pay me if I'm already there helping them with gathering. That day, I'll do a little extra—set up everything and help them afterwards, work out the drys or something like that. Basically, though, it's just everybody helps each other.

It's slower here in California. It's not so rushed a deal like working the big outfits in Nevada or Montana. You really got to hustle and get going there, because you got the weather to contend with and those big outfits just got to go a lot harder and push you like that. Here, they're trying to make money, too, but you just have more time it seems like and the weather is a lot easier. You can brand calves here in the middle of December, where up there you got to wait till spring. They probably brand calves here four months out of the year in easy weather.

Sometimes it takes them two or three days to gather. They bring them into little holding fields or whatever and then the day they brand, they work the cows off the calves and brand the calves. They'll turn in maybe fifteen calves and put in maybe four ropers and head

X Ranch, Kent, Texas.

and heel 'em. Then they'll turn them out and get some more. They brand their calves anywhere from three hundred to four hundred pounds. They head and heel everything here. They'll usually designate you a partner, and you two rope together.

CLAY BARTRAN, *Cowboy*
Tres Pinos, California

Out of everything in the brandin' pen, I'd just as soon flank. It's not something I'm gonna be able to do always and I'm gonna do it as long as I enjoy it and feel like doing it. Other than that, I'd just as soon run the knife. Course on top of all of it, I'd rather rope. But any of it, I don't care—run the dope bucket, I just enjoy it all.

I was lucky, my dad's cowboyed all his life and I had him for an example. I had a lot of older guys when I was young who told me a lot of stuff about do's and don'ts. Called my attention to it and woke me up. Like, don't ride in front of somebody. If you need to move

103

Cross HE Ranch, Lovington, New Mexico.

around the herd or even when you're being dropped off on a drive, you pull out. You go behind. You always hold your place. Wherever you're dropped off, that's where you should come out. If you get crossed up in the brush or something, when you come out, you get back where you're supposed to. Follow the drive leader, and don't ever get ahead or crowd him. Just a lot of good manners. When you're around a wagon, you learn pretty quick to stay out of the cook's way, where his territory is and where you get and don't get. Just like if you go to put your plate up and it's a windy day, you get around those fellows where you don't kick dirt in their plate and things like that.

I would watch somebody that I considered a good hand to know the do's and don'ts. One man might be better at something than another one and I'd just try to watch the good out of every man I considered a good hand. A lot of things you just learn by mistakes. You do it one way and it didn't work, so you'd try to figure out a better way to do it. I think bringing calves to the fire on the end of a rope is the easiest on cattle and it's an efficient way to do it. It's easier on everybody and it's more fun. You can work calves that way with less men than a lot of people use with a table. Course there's things to consider. You need some younger guys for calf flankers but there's men that get up fifty or so years old that don't mind flanking calves. But I don't favor a calf table, and, yes, I'd mind working for a place that used one.

A good outfit to one man might not be as good to another. But it's somebody that does things the way you think they ought to be done and you're comfortable that way. It's harmony in an outfit—the men get along. Somebody that's got respect for each other. And especially having respect for the man that runs it.

MIKE STEPHENS, *Cowboy*
Moorhouse Ranch Company
Gail, Texas

We moved to the Sam Hyatt Ranch in the Bighorn Mountains of Wyoming. They still fore-footed their colts, branded them, turned them out 'till they were three-, four-, or five-year-olds and then hired a rough string rider. Some of those colts weighed thirteen hundred pounds. I rode in the mountains and came in every week or two. My wife was fifty miles from town, so she didn't think it was as much fun as I did.

Between the Colorado and Wyoming jobs, I worked on a ranch in Albia, Iowa, that was pasturing cattle for the Waggoners during the drouth of the fifties in Texas. The cattle were a little wilder than Iowans were used to, so the boss asked if I could rope, since I'd been out West. I replied, "Well, the ones I don't miss."

There was an old cow with hoof rot that they hadn't been able to get in the pens. It had been raining a lot and I was using a grass rope that was sure stiff from the weather, so I threw as hard as I could. The rope just happened to go around her horns and figure-eight. She stepped in the bottom with both front feet and turned a flip. I had her stretched out, ready to doctor. The boss just stared and said, "I don't quite believe that." Of course, I never was able to do it again.

Wherever you are, I guess, there are things you wish you could change. There wasn't any way of advancing myself where I was. I knew I'd be a hired hand forever. I didn't particularly like working for other people, but I enjoyed the life. You have to make a trade-off somewhere. To me, a good cowboy has to be willing to do whatever it takes to make the cattle business work. It seems like everybody does it differently. There are about as many ways to make beef as there are ways to farm. We rope the calves as they are born, move cattle from pasture to pasture, cut pairs in the spring after they've calved, sort for shipping—all with horses. I have a hood off an old car that I dally to and pull behind my horse to bring in calves that get down in the snow. My wife says I use horses because I don't like to walk, but that's the only way I know how, I guess, and it seems to work for us. If I had to do this without horses, I'd put up the "for sale" sign.

CHARLIE SCHNECKLOTH, *Cowboy and rancher*
Maquoketa, Iowa

We run Hereford cows, a cow-calf operation. We've got a lot of brush country and some people don't like brush. The brush really isn't as big a problem after you learn to use it as it looks to be. But if you don't know how to use it, it can get pretty tough. We wear Levi jackets, most everybody wears shotgun chaps. No chinks in this country much at all. We dally most of the time. We use pretty stout horses in this country, we've got several Hancock horses. Almost all summer we run on national forest and Bureau of Land Management ground. In the spring, all the neighbors get together and we brand, I suppose, two or three thousand head. We heel the calves off their mothers. It's easier. We can have it done before you can get the calves cut off. We've got lots of experienced, good cowmen. We use two ropers and about six sets of wrestlers and three branders. It's about the only thing left that the neighbors all get together to do anymore.

We used to do everything together, used to hay, put up ice in the wintertime. Before we had electricity, we used to cut ice off the ponds and put it in ice houses, cover it up with sawdust. It would keep all summer. Then we'd get together and haul wood. Then we'd have a wood-sawing day and we'd all get together and saw wood. Times change and everybody got in a hurry and don't have time to help anybody else, I guess. That's one of the things that has put quite a burden on us. All the modern things that cost money, years ago we didn't have to have any of this. Now you have to have it. It just costs a lot more to live. I don't think we ever will give it up again. Too easy a life.

GEORGE TRACY, *Rancher and cowboy*
Campstool Ranch
Mayer, Colorado

We went out to Corral Lakes and stayed all night in an old cabin and it was forty-five degrees below zero up at the IL that night. You could see out between those boards and the snow was blowing in. Next morning, those poor horses were so cold, we couldn't hardly saddle them. We took off and I was riding a big long-legged bay horse and Hugh was riding a little sorrel horse. We were going along and pretty soon we run into three or four head of horses. We didn't want them very bad but we thought we'd follow them. All of a sudden, I looked around and Hughie wasn't behind me. I wondered what his idea of stopping was or if he had turned off. It was just foolish because I wouldn't know where he went. Snow was just a blowing and you couldn't see very far in any direction. I started backtracking but I was kind of losing the trail because the wind was blowing so bad. But every once in a while I could see a clump of snow piled out there. I looked down in this draw and it looked like a horse down there. I knew that couldn't be a wild horse, we'd gone up just a little while before. So I got off and turned over a sagebrush, so I could come back to my trail, and stuck it in the snow. I went down there and here was Hughie. He had this big pile of sagebrush

106

U Up and U Down Ranch, Fort Davis, Texas.

06 Ranch, Alpine, Texas.

and he was just sitting there, bare hands, with a match in them. I says, "Well, start the fire." "Naw," he says, "I don't want a fire. I'm not cold." I said, "Well, *I'm* cold. I'm going to start it anyway. So I reached in my pocket and finally got it going. He had it all fixed. It wasn't long when the fire got to going that he *was* cold. He just shook like a leaf.

We were out there running wild horses. We loved to run mustangs and that was the way we made our money to pay our taxes and make our living during the depression days. When I was a little kid five and six years old, I used to want to go with my dad and he would say, "You want to ride this horse? You want to ride that horse?" Some of them horses a little kid had no business on but I would try to ride them. I wanted to run mustangs with them, see, so I had to ride them horses. Six years old, I was. I run right over one cowboy. His horse fell down and I was right on his rear end when the horse went down, so I went right over the top and went right on. My dad put me up there and told me to go, and I did.

JOHN J. REED, *Buckaroo*
Willow Creek Ranch
Jiggs, Nevada

108

My horse had gone lame. I had one of those big boxes of matches in my chap pocket but when I got off to build that fire, my hands were too numb. I kept taking one out at a time and the wind was blowing them out. Pretty quick I piled them all in and they just smothered out. I knew I was in trouble. I thought I'd better run or do something, and I had a long McCarty so I tried running back and forth but that was scaring my horse. He was ten or twelve years old but I'd just started him about a month before that. There was no way I could get on that horse. I'd tried. He nearly got away from me so I got scared to run and I just set down. I'd given up. I had just set down there to freeze to death. I wasn't cold anymore and I was starting to get drowsy. If John hadn't of found me when he come back, I'd still be in there.

HUGH REED, *Buckaroo*
Lourence Ranch
Clover Valley, Nevada

One time we were up Tule Canyon and we were gathering cattle. Me and Roland Kilcrease and Bill Fowler went up one side of the canyon and you couldn't ride your horses, which didn't set too well with Roland. We got off and were walking our horses up, and there was about a foot and a half of snow on the ground and it was really coming down. We were all cold and wanting to go to the house but we were almost to the top. Finally Roland said, "I think we can ride from here," and he jumped on his horse. We went a little way up and his horse slipped and fell and Roland fell out of the saddle and his outside foot hung in the stirrup. His horse stood up and Roland was hanging upside down on his horse on the side of the mountain. We just walked on up there and he said in a real squeaky voice, "Would somebody please help me?"

It's pretty rough country and awful hard to get cattle off. And I'm sure not saying that the help we've had out here is not near enough cowboy to do it, because I think we've had some of the best. It's just one of those deals where you don't get them all gathered. A lot of these old cows that don't get picked up every year end up getting kind of wild, and some of them are not so much wild as they just got smart and know how to brush up. I'm sure there are cows that have been born and died here that have never been *seen*.

When Jingles first came to work out here we were up on Pine Peak and we were trying to get some cattle off up there, trying to move them to some lower country. We finally got up to where they were and took out after them. Jingles was in front of me and suddenly he just pulled up cussing. I asked him what was the matter and he said, "Those cows just disappeared. I was right here, right behind them, I could have touched them and I looked up and they were gone!" He was pretty upset and I told him he'd get used to that before it was all over with. I guess a feller could stay busy here year-round just running wild cattle.

Stake Ranch, Jiggs, Nevada.

Little Bear Ranch, Tres Pinos, California.

JD Ranch, Kent, Texas.

06 Ranch, Alpine, Texas.

When we're out looking for wild cattle, a lot of times we may spend a day or two or three just trying to find the area where the cattle are staying, riding waters and checking tracks. Once we kind of find what country they are in, we just go in and beat the brush until we find something. Then it depends on what the cattle do. If we can get around them and hold them up and drive them out, well, we'll sure do that first. But most of the time, as soon as they see you coming they're gone, and so *you're* gone and you just try to stay up with them until you get someplace where you can throw a loop and get one roped and snubbed to a tree. They'll usually lead better after they've been snubbed and left for a while. If we're close enough to get a trailer in there, we'll drag them up into a trailer and get them out that way. It's pretty hard to rope them up there and if you ever get to a place where you can swing a loop, you want to make sure it catches.

One time when I first came to work here, we were chasing seven or eight cows and had been after them for a week. We'd gotten two or three caught and finally one morning we hit the bunch of them. One cowboy had his dogs with him and they had the cattle held up so we rode in there and the cows took off. Everybody was going to get one roped and I was chasing this old high-horned cow and got to a place where I could throw a loop. I roped her and we were going a pretty good clip. About the time I got dallied off, I looked up and there was a big old spruce tree right in the middle of us. She went on one side and me and the horse went on the other and we almost met as she went around the tree and we went around the tree. But by the time we all got stopped, I had her tied to the tree.

RANDY GLOVER, *Cowboy*
U Up and U Down Ranch
Fort Davis, Texas

I remember the Appaloosa horse a friend of mine had so much trouble bridling. He always tried to beat him (get ahead of him, not hit him) to get the bit in his mouth and the bridle over his ears. We got the horse so he'd lower his head and if you just put the bridle on, that was fine. But if you tightened up and tried to do it fast, his head would go up. My friend was real intelligent, some kind of marine scientist, but when it came to feeling a horse, he couldn't do it. That quality wasn't there. He knew that the head was coming up and getting out of range, so he figured he'd beat him by speeding up. The horse would feel that every time and lift his head up. You can't try to beat 'em. I'd get the horse's head down there and get that ear forward and lift the headstall over the ear and over like that and—no problem. Then I'd say, "You do it." He never could get that. He was a real nice guy. He said once, "Every time I see someone bridle a horse easy, I want to buy that horse!"

ROY FORZANI, *Cowboy*
Law Ranch
Paicines, California

112

My granddad, John R. Morrell, homesteaded up north of Paonia and acquired about twelve thousand acres of land. He ran yearlings and had a cow-calf operation. He sold the land to my dad and his brother. Then this coal company came in and bought my dad's cows, forest permit, and about sixteen hundred acres. So I went to work for them. There's no big cow operations left. You can't make a living at it. Cattle prices haven't come up with the economy. When they went to mining coal, coal miner's wages were so high, your average ordinary cowboy making six or seven hundred dollars a month could hardly live. Everything's going up, cattle prices are staying the same.

The worst part about this country is the winters. The pasture snows under so you have to feed them so long and it takes a lot of money, buying that much hay. We'll raise about nine hundred ton of hay up here and it will take about twelve hundred to winter the cows. But this country is probably the easiest there is in Colorado. I've seen it twenty-five below up here but it doesn't stay, maybe four or five days. But the snow stays. The first year I was here, we had three feet that stayed on all winter, but the average is about two foot. We move the cows down lower. The worst part is when you're calving. There'll be mud under the snow and it's kind of tough to keep those calves alive. We'll have about one hundred and fifty first-calf heifers and we'll have to keep them in the pen pretty close and watch them. Make sure they aren't having any trouble. We might have to pull a calf if one can't have it. She'll lay down and strain and strain and maybe her water sack will break and you can tell within a few hours if she's going to have it. If she can't, we'll run her in and pull the calf. We have one of your average calf pullers. They set on the back of the cow and you hook chains to the calf's legs and just crank it right out. It's basically a come-along type deal. Cows usually won't have as much trouble as heifers, maybe one backwards or has a leg turned back.

The cows, we try to go through them at least once a night and then ride through them in the daytime. Make sure nothing is having trouble. What we try to do within a day or two is match-tag them with their moms to where they're easily paired up. Not much sleep. We stay out all day. And then we try to check the heifers every two hours day and night, so you don't want to get used to sleeping much. After about sixty days it gets kind of tiring. It lasts about sixty days. But if it lasted any longer than that, I'd probably stay with it. Yeah, try to save all the calves you can.

Can't say there's any part I don't like but some I like better than others. Riding through the brush gathering them isn't all it's cracked up to be, but you have to take the good with the bad. They told me if you could cowboy up here in Terror Creek, you could cowboy anywhere. The way I look at it, the Lord put people on the earth to do certain jobs and I guess he put me here to take care of cattle. That's all I've ever done. I would say it's worth it, but I don't know if I'll always be able to do it. It will depend a lot on the economy. They've got this ranch up for sale right now.

MONTE MORRELL, *Cowboy*
Seven X Ranch
Hotchkiss, Colorado

Pitchfork Land and Cattle Company, Guthrie, Texas.

I was born in Burley, Idaho, but I was raised in northern Nevada and southern Idaho and western Montana and now California. I worked at the Spanish Ranch in Tuscarora, Nevada, and I spent a lot of time for Simplot's in Idaho and Nevada and—gosh, I could go on all day. I'm interested in the horses, the California-style reined cow horse, and I wanted to come to California and learn more about it.

This is where it originally started from and this is where it all happens. I like this country real well. They're not in such a hurry to get their cattle work done. They've got time, if you want to putter with your horse. They like their horses here and they kind of put their horses on a pedestal. That's kind of what I like instead of just ramming and jamming your horse and getting your cattle worked, not enough hours in the day. It's not that way down here so bad, the old California style. In the old days they had a lot of time to play with their horses and everybody really prided theirself in riding good horses. It's still that way down here, even in this day and age. People still take a lot of pride in their horses. It's tradition and it's just a good feeling to ride a good horse. These people, they like lots of silver and pride themselves on their equipment. I've worked a lot of places where, heck, they use baling wire and a long-shanked snaffle to hold their headstall on and get just as much done but they don't take the pride in themself that people down here do. There's good hands anywhere you go but they have different styles of working cattle, different ways of doing things. But in their own way, they're all good hands. I'm not really partial.

JESS BRACKENBURY, *Cowboy*
Tres Pinos, California

114

We use a chuck wagon in the fall and spring when we're working and the reason we do, it's the most efficient way we have of working this country. We're in the cow business. It's our only form of income and we watch the expenses real close. We don't use a chuck wagon for the romance part of it. And it's not that we're a big ranch, but on these lease outfits we can pull in there with a truckload of horses and a chuck wagon and set up camp and go to work. We keep our groceries and our horses close to where we are working. We get a lot done in a hurry and then move on to the next place and keep going. We've expanded our operation in recent years and we've always camped around at different places, but what is known as a chuck wagon, it's just been in the last ten or fifteen years that we've started doing that. It works real well for us. It's a little different than the ones on these big ranches. Ours is mounted on rubber wheels and we might pull it a hundred miles for a week and work somewhere and then pull it another fifty miles to another place.

We don't have a real big crew. We don't ever work over eight men in the fall or the spring and we don't make real big drives. It's brushy country. We stay close together and make several drives in one pasture and don't brand any big number of calves at one time. A hundred calves is normally about as many as we ever brand at one brandin', sometimes maybe two hundred. The brush slows us down, it takes longer to work, and on the lease ranches we can't control the brush because of the expense. So that's the reason we use a chuck wagon. If you've got a little bitty outfit and use a wagon and it's not economical, then you're putting it in a category with playing polo or team roping or something. Which, if you want to spend your money doing that, that's fine. But we think it's the best way for us to work. We watch our expenses.

TOM MOORHOUSE, *Rancher and cowboy*
Moorhouse Ranch Company
Benjamin, Texas

One time Dean Tobias and I took a government contract and we run horses for the government. We gathered up nine hundred and seventy of them on that contract. On a government contract like that, you bid it. I think four other people bid on that contract and we were the lowest bidders. They give us a two-part contract. One part was to gather two hundred head and I think we bid it fifty-six dollars a head. And the other part was to gather seven hundred and seventy and we bid them at fifty-four dollars. That's to go out and gather the horse and haul him to Reno to the holding facility at Palomino Valley.

Tobias and I had another partner who furnished the helicopter. The government won't let you use anything but a helicopter to run them. So one of us would ride with the helicopter pilot because he didn't know how to handle horses or livestock. We used the helicopter just like you would a saddle horse, only a helicopter doesn't ever get tired. You would just build a trap somewhere where you think the horses will go in. We'd gather up a bunch of horses and by the time we got them close to the trap, we'd have them handling well enough that you could turn them or stop them, pretty well set them up the way you needed to. Then you'd go to the trap. Most of the time they'd go in, sometimes they wouldn't. We'd have a ground crew there on saddle horses and if they spilled out of the wings, then we'd rope them and tie them down. If there were more horses got away than there were riders, the guy in the helicopter would hold the loose ones up till the riders had time to rope them. After everything was caught, you'd go back and let them up and take them to the trap. The last two traps we had, we corralled three hundred in each trap.

We used Powder River panels. No, you don't camouflage them, but you do to a certain extent. One trap was in real high sagebrush, sagebrush as high as you are on a horse. It was in the bottom of a draw and there was a real deep gully there that we used as one wing. Then we built a wing off the gully and had the trap setting right on the edge of this gully. That worked real good. Your trap is the most important thing. That determines whether you're going to get them in or not. The second trap we set up didn't work worth a hoot. We had a lot of trouble with it and we roped all the horses that we gathered there. It was just a bad trap. The horses knew it and they wouldn't go in.

The government's got no business in the horse business. I'll tell it the way I think it is. If they don't like it, too bad! Before the government stepped in there, the horses were controlled and the ranchers made money controlling them. Now the government steps in and they say *they* control them, but they've increased. I think when they passed the law in 1971, there was like nine thousand horses in Nevada and right now there's like forty thousand. So they're not controlling them and they're losing money doing it. There used to be horse runners in different parts. If the horses built up in one area, they would go in there and maybe they'd get two or three ranchers to go with them and gather those horses until they got them down to where the ranchers could live with them. They'd always leave some for seed. It wasn't like they were going to make them extinct, because they didn't want to cut their own throat either. They knew that if they took them all, there wouldn't be any there in ten years for them to gather again, see. If that's the way you make your living, you don't cut your own throat. And they made money at it.

The government's losing a lot of money. Just like us there. We bid that contract for fifty-six dollars. That's what it cost the government for us to gather them and put them in the holding facility. And then they had to brand them and work them and sort them and I don't know how much they were in them. They have the adoption program going and they were giving the horses away for twenty-five dollars a horse, those nine hundred and seventy we gathered. If you wanted to adopt a horse, you paid the government twenty-five dollars a horse. If it cost them fifty-six just to get him into the corrals, then they give him away for twenty-five, that's not too good of arithmetic. So they could see they were losing a lot of money. Then they jacked the price up to two hundred. Well, then they couldn't get rid of the horses. According to government law, you can't chicken-feed them, so they were just keeping them there for twenty years, till they died. It cost them all that feed and they weren't doing anybody any good. So then they lowered it down to one hundred twenty-five dollars and that's where it is now, the way I understand it.

The horse runners chicken-fed them. They'd start a few of them and use them for their own use and the ranchers would keep a few. I neighbored with a guy down here and I'll bet ninety percent of his cavvy was mustangs. They're good horses. On that contract, one bunch of horses we gathered up were good quality horses. They were over there by the Circle A and they would turn out thoroughbred studs. They'd have made real good saddle horses. That's what a mustang is: a rancher's cavvy, brood mare bunch, just turned wild. Some of them they didn't get gathered. They would go out and take care of them and gather them up and keep their feet trimmed down. They knew that if they got too many, they'd be without grass. There's no difference at all between them and any other horse that has been range-raised when you're breaking them.

RANDY STOWELL, *Buckaroo*
Currie, Nevada

06 Ranch, Alpine, Texas.

Cross HE Ranch, Lovington, New Mexico.

My wife and I have had a camp job on a ranch somewhere for practically all of the fifteen years we've been married. Like any cowboy, I've always wanted a little bunch of cows of my own and a little place to run them. After waiting around for several years, we were finally able to buy a little twenty-acre piece of ground and lease around a section of country that joins up with it where we can run a few head of yearlings. It's a pretty poor kind of an outfit. We just got outside fence, and not very much of that. No facilities, no pens at all. So when we work cattle it's out in the pasture, and if we have to use a set of pens we have to go through a neighbor and use some of his or make do the best we can.

I got to thinking about Ray Hunt's techniques on teaching horses to load in trailers. It was all a matter of getting a horse to yield to pressure, making the right thing easy and the wrong thing difficult. So I got the idea that if a feller really needed to, he could load a cow or a yearling or a bull or any other kind of critter in a trailer just as easy as he could load a horse in a trailer. It's all the same principle. So I didn't see any reason why a feller couldn't load his cattle in a trailer in the middle of a pasture if he could load his horse in a trailer in the middle of a pasture. It was just a matter of having the patience and taking the time to do it.

The first time I ever used the idea was a couple of years ago when I had a little handful of yearlings I needed to get out of my lease pasture and move somewhere else. I didn't have any help (my wife was off taking pictures of other cowboys), no portable pens or anything. I

118

Chilicote Ranch, Valentine, Texas.

just pulled my pickup and trailer up close to a fence, gathered my yearlings and worked them a little bit until I got them ready to load. Then I just drove them up in the trailer horseback.

In order to load any kind of a cow brute in a trailer, she's got to feel like that's the best place to go. If she don't want to go in there, you're not going to get her in there short of using force and dragging her in there with a winch. But if you can get the idea across to cattle that a good place to be is that trailer, well, there's nothing in the world that will stop them from going in there.

So when I've got a handful of yearlings to load, I'll try to first have them handling a little bit. That's pretty much essential on the kind of operation I've got, to get my cattle handling where a feller can bend them a little and drive them where he wants to. When you've got that done, the hard part is over. So I'll gather my yearlings and I'll drive them around a little bit and get them where they're wanting to stick together and drive them up to the trailer. When they walk up to it and kind of accept it, I'll back off from them and let them stand there if they want to. If they want to go on by the trailer and leave out, I'll just circle around them and get them stopped and point them back toward the trailer. Then when they start back toward it, I quit driving and quit pushing on them.

If they go by it again, I'll circle around them and get them stopped again and point them back toward it and pretty soon they'll stop around the trailer. When they do that, I'll just ride off and give them a little air and let them think it over. Pretty soon the idea comes across that that's the best place in the world they can be. The pressure is all off of them there, and the right thing is real easy. If they do the wrong thing and wander off or go on by the trailer another time, things get difficult.

But pretty soon whenever they're stopping and standing right there at the trailer and relaxing a little bit, then I can wad them up and drive them around behind it and drive them right in there. When you get your animals headed in some general direction of where you want them to go, you got to sure enough remember not to put any pressure on them there. I've seen so many cowboys get an animal headed toward a gate and then they really build to 'em, go to hollering and whipping and crowding on them. Pretty quick they've got that animal where he'll spin right around and run off. Maybe if they just got him to look toward the gate and then back off, sit and give him air, he might just drift right through there on his own. As quick as you start putting pressure on that animal, he thinks, "Well, what I'm doing is wrong. I've got to do something different and get the hell out of here." He ain't about to go through the gate then unless he just does it accidentally.

So when you get these cattle up next to the trailer, get them headed that way and wanting to go through it, that's where you want to quit on them. You get them with their nose right in the gate and then you make a big run at them and holler and squall and whip them on the rear, and you're going to drive them right *out* of there. And then you might not get them back to the trailer because they already figured out things get tough when they are there. There's a lot of common sense involved. You got to make it easy for them to go up there and do right and difficult when they turn around and leave. That takes all the work out of it.

If they're a little bit trotty or hard to handle, I might unhook my pickup and drive it around and pull it up to the end of the trailer gate and make a wing with the pickup on one side and a wing out of the fence on the other side. If a feller's just got one old bull to load or one cow or one pair or a yearling, then you wouldn't even need to be around a fence. In fact a fence might even get in your way, because there's no problem keeping *one* animal together. That reminds me of Ron Goddard saying a lady once asked a feller if one cow could stampede. The old feller thought about it a minute and said, "Yes ma'am. One cow can stampede, but one cow can't scatter." Where you're apt to scatter a bunch, then a fence is pretty handy to have.

JOEL NELSON, *Cowboy*
o6 Ranch
Alpine, Texas

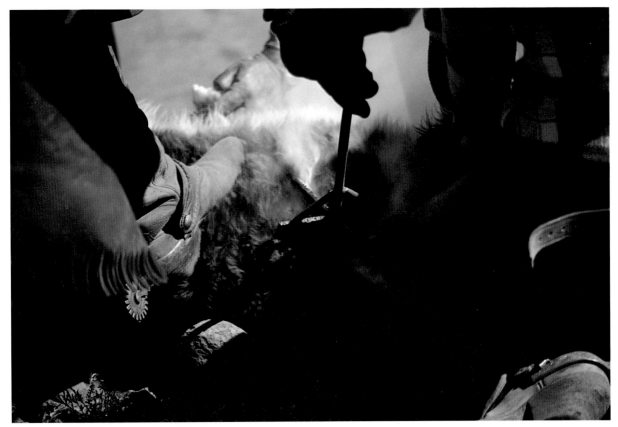

X Ranch, Kent, Texas.

First Continental Corporation Ranch, Winnett, Montana.

I wanted to be a cowboy from a little kid. I can't remember wanting to be anything else. I was raised on a ranch and I don't know how I got the idea that I wanted to break horses, but I had that idea from when I was real small.

I was very, very fortunate to be neighbor to Bill Dorrance. He's kind of my earliest hero. Everything he did was the best of anybody in that country. He was the best roper, best horseman, rawhided, good cowboy. So he was kind of my hero. I went to work for Bill when I got out of college. Stayed there five and a half months, wasn't getting any pay or anything, just for what I could learn. Then I heard about Ray Hunt and Tom Dorrance from him. Ray called one day and wanted to know if I could help him. I didn't take any wages there with him either—worked for nothing for a while. He kept talking about Bill's brother Tom and about Nevada. So I went to Nevada and started horses for the Spanish Ranch over there and it wasn't very good pay but the horses were the most challenging that I thought I would ever run into. There were a lot of six- and seven-year-olds and eight-year-olds. They were thoroughbred horses and full grown. I started a lot of them five different years. Then I had a chance to go to work with Tom Dorrance, working for a guy in California that bought

Cowan Cattle Company, Big Sandy, Montana.

nineteen colts from the Twenty-Five. I worked with them three guys in between working with myself.

I probably taught myself more than those guys ever did but I wouldn't have been able to if they hadn't got me started. You work this philosophy and I tell you, you can do just about anything that's physically possible. Make the right things easy, the wrong things difficult. Get so you can recognize and settle for the slightest try. It's like Ray says, "It's L–I–F–E." It's just life. You can't make a cow get through a gate. If she doesn't want to go, the only way I know is to latch on to her with your rope and drag her through maybe. But you can't force. It's got to be *her* idea to go through there. If you see some dudes or guys that aren't too handy, they'll try to force her through and she'll just plow through their horse and lose respect and then you can't do nothing with her. But if you ease her around there and get her to look, why, you can run her down a badger hole if she'd fit.

You might start out with a bull and he's plowing through the cows and he's leaving the country. You just keep blocking him, blocking him, and he'll keep going around your horse and around your horse. But pretty soon he'll turn away from your horse. And that's the slightest try. You build on that. He turns away from your horse one time and you just stop your horse and sit there. Just let him drift. It doesn't matter if he drifts a little bit and then goes back, you still let him drift. Then pick him up again. It won't be long, he'll turn away from your horse again. It's easy to make the wrong things difficult for a bull. Then you get a little handle on him so that you can bend him and he knows that if he yields, you'll back off. Then you just keep building on that. I've loaded a lot of bulls into a trailer alone in the middle of a pasture on a three-year-old colt. I sure couldn't have drug him in there, no way. I've never loaded more than one at a time but I'm sure you could do it.

Heck, you can do anything if you work this philosophy. Just like if you got a cow in the loading chute and maybe she's the last cow and she's broke back two or three times. You can't get her to go up the loading chute. Most people, she'll be ramming around there and when she takes the loading chute, that's when they buzz her. I tell those truck drivers to just leave their hotshots alone. When her tail's pointed toward the loading chute, then buzz her, but everybody back off when she goes up toward the truck. That's the hardest thing to get truck drivers to do. They want to buzz 'em when they're going up in there 'cause they can reach 'em good, see. But heck, it's just the opposite of the way it works. It don't matter if it's a horse, dog, cow, little kids, it all works the same. It's like Ray says, "It's life!"

BRYAN NEUBERT, *Buckaroo*
Robert R. Marvel Ranches
Lamoille, Nevada

06 Ranch, Alpine, Texas.

After I gave up the leather reins and got to using the rawhide reins with the romal, I never wanted to go back. It seemed like they were just more fitting to my way of life. Now I know that you don't have to have rawhide reins to go out and accomplish a real good job, and every horse doesn't have to be handled with what we call "the old California style" to get the job done. I've seen some real good horses and good men who had split reins and a grazer bit and a lot of things were different, but the men understood their horse and they understood the animal they were working. So they were right up at the top. It just kind of depends on where you come from as to how things got started.

It has always been interesting to me to watch other people when they are handling horses or when they are working with cattle, and especially roping. I really enjoy roping—never did rope at the rodeos, rodeo style. Sort of had a one-man ranch and I never had a lot of time. It seemed like it took all my time to keep things going on the ranch and to get my horses working a little better.

When heading and heeling in the branding pen, there is one heel throw that I used to use when starting to rope on a colt. The animal did not want to let you get up close to it, so you would let the animal run around a little bit until it settled and the head man got it set up. You then could throw what I call a "flank shot." You are directly out to the right side of the hindquarters with a fair-sized loop and you throw it straight in there. If you were right-handed, you'd be on a right-hand side of the animal, directly to the side of the hindquarters. You can be out there quite a ways and you pitch that loop right straight at them. It's an underhand shot, you throw it underhanded and you let it get straightened out way out behind you. Your shoulder rolls back and when you bring your loop forward, your elbow bends a little, so that loop comes right straight by you and goes right straight out. If you're on the target, the lower end of your loop—the back end—it slides right in underneath as the other part goes over the hip and it hangs up there. If you get it on exactly right, that part that goes over the hip, it'll come back and under their tail. For a few seconds you'll have a figure-eight around both feet and the tail. Usually you don't try for that, it just happens that way. You've got a good chance to come up with both hind feet, but most always one. It's a good shot on a colt, you don't have to run your colt after the animal and you don't have to get him all messed up while getting started.

Just about everybody gets the job done one way or another, but when I was riding colts and took a colt into a branding corral for the first time, I liked to just throw at the hind feet. I'd go up directly behind a calf and throw when it was standing. When you dallied, you didn't have to dally fast since your horse already knew how to back up. The other fellow, of course, pulled him ahead just as that loop went in under there so your horse didn't get all bothered. I've had plenty of horses and seen plenty of horses that were really bothered when they came into the branding corral the first time. The fire was bothering to them, everything was bothering to them. But, if you just took a little time with them and just worked the hind end to start with, before the day was over, you'd never know they'd been bothered to start with. Before the day was over, of course, you'd be throwing at the head too and you'd be dragging the calves on up to the fire.

Mountain Island Ranch, Glade Park, Colorado.

MC Ranch, Adel, Oregon.

MC Ranch, Adel, Oregon.

Chilicote Ranch, Valentine, Texas.

I've never been any place yet where they didn't get the job done, one way or another, sooner or later. But a lot of it was certainly done the hard way and the fellows certainly didn't intend to be doing it the hard way, but it was the only way they knew to do it.

BILL DORRANCE, *Horseman*
Dorrance Ranch
Salinas, California

What am I doing? Sometimes I wonder about that myself. I'm making a living running cattle—steers this time, a little over a thousand on about two hundred thousand acres. There's new management here and they don't even know what they have. So we're running a herd of cattle here on their property and getting to know as much as we can this year so they'll know what their potential is for the future. I'd say we've been successful. A lot of people around here said that we wouldn't even have any steers left when we came out of this country. We don't have them all, but we know where they are—we've got 'em.

This is my first time on a large steer operation. They're kind of silly, like a bunch of teenagers. But I've got a good crew and we've handled them real well. I was here when we received them off the trucks last winter, fed them and doctored them. We've cowboyed on them now for six months and they handle good, real good. I like working steers. They're sort of the Cadillac of cattle in my opinion. They don't bellar as much when you're moving them, they're easier to move, they walk better and don't heat up as fast. Of course it's better in the morning, but you can gather them in the middle of the day—where a cow, lots of times, if she's at a water hole and her calf is off somewhere else, you've got to get them mothered before you can go. You don't have to mother steers. Once they get walking, they really walk. We've had these steers strung out for two miles or so, all of them walking.

Things happen, but you expect things to happen. Nobody's been hurt. A lot of it is rough, a lot of it isn't very well fenced. We didn't know the boundaries, nobody knew all the boundaries when we came into this country. We've been out here six months or so and still haven't seen a lot of it. But we know the potential now. We have to anticipate the steers before we go into a country and try to anticipate what they're going to do, where they're going to go and where we're going to find them. So far, we've been right. We've been snowed on and rained on and heated on but we didn't really mind it. Wet and cold, that happens, but we expect that. Horses have held up real well, they're in good shape. We always make sure that they get plenty to eat because they have to work hard. We give them as much time off as we can. Some of them are getting a little leg-weary and we could use a few more. We stay in this tent, right here. My family is right here and we're a team. Best home I ever had—that and my saddle.

BILL DUGAN, *Cowboy and contract wagon boss*
Nye, Montana

Rancho La Rosita, Muzquiz, Coahuila, Mexico.

U Up and U Down Ranch, Fort Davis, Texas.

06 Ranch, Alpine, Texas.

I was born in Colorado and I've worked from Arizona to Alaska, from Colorado to Korea and everywhere in between. In that Mitchell Oregon country, we use dogs for just about everything, mostly head dogs—border collies, kelpies and McNabs. We've still got a couple of old heelers and one of them thinks he's a head dog. He'll kind of work around in front. This one kelpie we've got, one day we were moving cows and calves and they went through a field that had some bulls in it. He just kept the cows and calves going through and sorted them right past the bulls and never even bothered them. I don't know if he did it on purpose or not, but that's how it happened. We train our own—or they train us.

I think the best way to get along with a dog is just work with him the best way you can, don't try and make him work your way. You just have to watch him, and if he isn't doing things exactly your way but you are getting where you want to go, maybe just kind of go along with him and let him do his thing. Good dogs that work cattle, why they'll *want* to do her. If they catch on to where you're going, they'll get the job done. You might not think they're doing her right, but if you just stand back and give them a little air, they'll generally get her done. There's a lot of good dogs and a lot of not-so-good-dogs. Maybe if you had a not-so-good dog, you wouldn't want to do that, I don't know. But they've all had their shiny days. Once in a while you wonder why you have any of them, and then about the time you think you ought to get rid of the whole works, why they really do a good job.

When we were in Alaska and had brown bear problems, we had heelers then. When a bear would have a cow, eating it in an alder patch, they'd stand there and look into it, but you couldn't get them to go in there. So they was thinking, too. They stayed out. A kelpie we had with us there, he didn't like bears and he'd point them out to you. He'd make a circle around them and go to barking and raising cain and show you where they were. He knew they were the outsiders, the guys that you didn't need around.

DOC MUNSON, *Buckaroo*
Fitzgerald Ranch
Mitchell, Oregon

MC Ranch, Adel, Oregon.

06 Ranch, Alpine, Texas.

First Continental Corporation Ranch, Winnett, Montana.

Mountain Island Ranch, Glade Park, Colorado.

We have five thousand acres, lots of brush to pop, and run about three hundred and fifty mother cows. This year we ran about three hundred yearlings also. We work horseback and ride quite a bit, although we don't just strictly cowboy all the time. We have a team of work horses to help feed in the winter. I have worked on some ranches in Texas, Nebraska sand hills, Wyoming and New Mexico; so I am aware of what a cowboy job is.

MARLIN TRUMMEL, *Rancher and cowboy*
Stockton, Missouri

One time we rode up on Elk Basin. The grass was getting short and we needed to move the cattle. Here were cow and calf elk mixed with cow and calf Herefords. We sat there in a little while wondering how to separate them, but all we had to do was yell.

MAX PUCKETT, *Cowboy*
CA Ranch
Bozeman, Montana

132

CHAPTER FIVE

CRAFTSMEN

*The quality that only shows when
you know what to look for*

I STEPPED OFF THE PLANE in the Reno airport wearing my usual faded jeans, cotton shirt and dust-and-rain-spotted hat. The well-dressed airport set tried not to walk close enough to make anyone think they knew me. The ladies in spiked heels and matching handbags were probably wondering where I even got the money to buy a plane ticket.

Things like that don't bother me much. I'm not into teetering or handbags, so there was very little envy on my part or theirs. But watching them did remind me that I hadn't been taking very good care of my comfortable boots, so I stepped up on an old, black, gray-haired shoeshiner's chair and asked for a shine. He turned up the cuff of my jeans and said, "Mercers?" I was amazed. Yes, they were Mercers but I was about two thousand miles from the dusty little boot shop on South Chadbourne Street in San Angelo, Texas, where Weaver took my measurements and Mr. Lopez put them together by hand. "How did you know?" I asked.

"In my business, you don't make a living off the people who wear Thom McAn shoes." I sat there as he soaped and scrubbed and treated my boots with the care most people only give a newborn child. His price was a dollar and a half a shine, but his leather products were imported from England, the best money could buy. "Why don't you use cheaper leather products," I asked, "and give yourself a bigger profit?"

"Well," he patiently explained to this terribly nosy lady, "my customers are people like you. When they spend four hundred to two thousand dollars on what they wear on their feet, they know the difference. By doing the best job I can do and using the best products, that's the way I stay in business. I don't like to punch a clock. I like to be my own boss."

Saddle by Dale Harwood, Shelley, Idaho.

I sat and watched the three-piece crowd go by. Only one person in that two-story airport knew I was wearing Weaver's handmade Mercer boots, probably the most expensive footgear in the place. And as they walked by us, I'm sure they only saw an old shoeshine boy in the world's lowliest job.

It's funny how few people really know quality when they see it, and how a little pride can transform a laborer into a craftsman.

I moved to Elko from Texas seven years ago. I started building saddles ten years ago and I've been on my own now for about two years. I worked in Fort Worth at Ryon's a couple years and then I moved up here to go to work for Capriola's and worked there three and a half years.

If a guy wanted to be a top trainer, horse trainer or something, Elko probably wouldn't be the place. The climate's not for it. You could go to California or Texas, where there's lots of top trainers and see what other people are doing and you don't get stuck in a rut. You don't get to thinking, "That's good enough." But when I moved up here, there's quite a few good saddlemakers and leatherworkers around. It was my nature to try to get better anyway, but when you see lots of things that are really nice, you realize it is possible to do that. This has a climate for good handicrafts: rawhide and silver and leather. If it is competition, it's friendly competition. The people around here demand it, too. That's what they like to see. They're getting used to it. I don't know how something like that gets started in a place, but it seems like once it does, it goes pretty good. It's a pride in yourself.

I guess my name's getting spread around a little more all the time. I don't know what else you could hope for. Something like that is something to be proud of, to me. I just try to make each one a little bit better—try to make something that will fit a little bit better, be a little more comfortable or help the rider in whatever way I can. I just keep trying to make each one better than the last. I don't really know why, just my nature, I suppose. My customers are nobody particularly famous, just the working guys around here mostly. It's the clientele I'm comfortable with. I understand them better. I understand how they think and how they work and how they live. You get some big money people come in, and they have a different outlook on things. Lots of times it's awful hard to communicate with them. And it's real hard to communicate through a saddle to them. I like building saddles for the working guy. They're appreciative. An owner or a manager of a place, when he sees half of his crew riding a saddle that was built by the same guy, and some good hands too, when his friends start looking for a saddle, he's going to remember that. That's kind of how things spread around. I've seen quite a few times when a guy on a crew will order a saddle from me and within a year, there will be quite a few of them riding my saddles, too. Kind of like they all get the bug when they see something they like.

I know a couple of older guys that I think were getting kind of discouraged thinking things were going to die out and now there's coming along a generation that seems interested in carrying things on. The older guys were always just more than happy to show you, or tell you what they knew about something. It's the same way with horsemanship too. I really think young guys now, there are a lot more of them trying to do things right instead of just any old way.

I'll start to get in a rut after a year or so and find there's a lack of things I see that I can improve on. So I'll go see Dale Harwood. He's the kind of guy—you may not even talk about saddles. You may talk about something completely different, but somehow or another he sparks thinking in you. When you come home you feel fresh, and all of a sudden you see things that you never saw before in your work. He's got something that sparks your thinking process. He's encouraging, but at the same time he warns you that it's not easy. He lets you know you're in for some work. But, "You can do it. Shoot, there's not that much to it." He's just kind of that way.

That was one thing I really liked when I came up here. A saddlemaker was somebody that was respected. A saddle was something that was respected. Most of these guys have more pride in their saddle than they do in their pickup or whatever else they've got. So the guy that made it is an important person to them, too. That respect is kind of nice to have.

SCOTT BROWN, 29, *Saddlemaker*
Elko, Nevada

Large mecate by Blind Sam, Colingo, California. Small mecates
and hobbles by Fred Dorrance, San Juan Bautista, California.

Riata made and held by Merlin Rupp, Rock Creek Ranch, French Glen, Oregon.

I 've done quite a bit of braiding. My dad gave me the desire. He used to braid when he was younger. He made more ropes than he did anything. As I was a kid growing up, I'd hear him talk about it. He'd show all us boys how to braid four-, six-, eight- and twelve-plait. But by the time I got old enough that I wanted to learn how to braid, learn to tie the buttons and what not, he'd forgotten. He used to know all the buttons, too. So I learned mine out of a book. I just wanted to make my own gear. It's a little neater to be able to say that you made most of the stuff you use rather than bought it. And then you can make different styles. You can do your own thing. It isn't the same as everybody else's on the wagon. You've got something that they don't have. It's just like people putting chrome on their pickup or their car: that's why they do it, to get it a little better or more unique than the guy's next door. That's a cowboy, I guess. I make my own cinches. I've made them from mohair and horsehair both. I twist McCartys. I make my own leggin's, headstalls, reins—rawhide reins. My main thing now is leather hackamores.

RANDY STOWELL, *Buckaroo*
Cordano Ranch
Currie, Nevada

All I'd ever done was buckaroo and ranch. I'd always wanted a few cows and some ground of my own, but when I finally got them I couldn't afford to make a living on them. I drove a truck for a little while but that didn't work. I wrecked a couple of those. So I just decided on silversmithing. I melt sterling silver in like it was brazing rod. It becomes part of the metal. All is welded in. I do it on spurs, for instance, when the band is flat and then bend them afterwards and the silver just stays. It is part of it. It helps strengthen the piece and I use my own scraps. I guarantee my silver to stay on and I've never replaced any yet. I would look at engraving that I liked, try to reproduce the cuts that I wanted and work out my own patterns. I bought a book about engraving but the only thing I got out of it was that engraving was a form of art and it was up to the artists how they did it. What worked, I did again. What didn't work, I didn't do again.

MARK DAHL, *Bit and spur maker*
Deeth, Nevada

138

Silver inlay by Art Harsin, Enterprise, Oregon.

Well, my method isn't much different than a lot of others except that first of all I stretch the hide in a frame until dry and then scrape the hair off instead of soaking it and taking it off. By having it in the frame with the hair off, when you hold it up to the light you see all the grub spots that are healed and don't show unless you had it stretched. I mark all those spots so when I cut the string out, as I pass one of those spots I can trim it out. That eliminates a lot of weak spots in your string.

After that string is cut out and stretched, I then throw it in and soak it up again and get it good and wet and flesh it down to the thickness that it needs to be. Then I take it out and string it along the fence and look it over once more on each side for any spots I might have missed. Sometimes after you clean that string off there will be a spot show up that you would not have seen otherwise. I believe that is what makes the better riata. I've had many fellows tell me, "You don't get many hides that make a good riata." But I've found there are quite a lot of hides that will make a good riata if you get all the weak spots out of it before you start to braid the string. But if there is a weak spot in the string—I'd a lot rather put a splice in it when I'm braiding than to have to put one in after I have it braided. If you make a good riata, you've got to braid it tight and when you go to splicing one of those tight riatas later on, then you've got a real job on your hands.

Some people think you have to pull hard when braiding, but you don't pull any harder than you push. You push back on those crosses to get them to set up. If you get them braided tight, that's what makes your riata stand up good after it gets worn. I first learned from my brother Fred and a fellow that he worked with and they kind of wanted it to look natural. They never rolled their rawhide after it was braided, but they might tap it just a little bit to smooth it up and get the crosses to set down nicely. They liked their rawhide to look as much as possible like it did in the string before it was braided. They liked to see it have a crest on the top. I just got in the habit of doing it that way and that's the kind that looks the nicest to me today: the most natural look.

When the hide is soaked in something to loosen the hair up, usually the soaking will change the rawhide color. If you scrape it off when it's dry, you get the true look of rawhide. But everybody has their own opinion of what looks best to them. I never put anything on it until I get ready to use it. It will last a lot longer if it isn't soaked up in fat or oil. You never put oil on rawhide as it will soften it up and cause it to deteriorate. Fat will make it slick and you just want it slick on the outside. I don't put anything but raw beef fat on them and I just do that when I've been using them. Sometimes I put a little on my hand and then rub my hand over the rawhide. If I'm out where they get wet or they get real muddy, I'll wash all the mud off and let them get good and dry. I'll then put a little heavier coat of fat on them. The flank makes a good fat, it seems to have more tissue in it and is not so tallow-like. The bag fat off a heifer is also good.

It wasn't easy for me to learn the different patterns of the buttons. I wasn't working at it that steady. But I learned how to get the strings right, work with the right amount of moisture in them and to gauge them true. You learn to get a good feel of a string if you have a good string to work with. I've worked some string that wasn't good and it is a lot more difficult to work and get it so it's fairly serviceable and just fair looking. You've got to pull those strings a little different, those that aren't so strong. But if you have a good piece of rawhide and get your strings made true, then the braiding isn't too difficult.

BILL DORRANCE, *Horseman*
Dorrance Ranch
Salinas, California

Boots by Paul Bond, Nogales, Arizona.
Spurs by Melton McCowan, Hamilton, Montana.

Top reins and quirt by Fred Dorrance, San Juan Bautista, California. Other reins by Bill Dorrance, Salinas, California. Bosals by Ernie Ladouceur, Madera, California.

I started off by going to a one-year saddlemaker school in Amarillo, Texas, and ran out of money after nine months and went traveling. That's really when I started learning the most, because that's when I got to see how much I *didn't* learn in school. I worked for two weeks for a fellow in Casper, Wyoming; worked for four hours for a fellow in Billings, Montana, and for an hour and a half for a saddlemaker in Belle Fourche, South Dakota. Then I went to work for Chuck Stormes in Calgary for six and a half years.

When I was in school it was kind of the general attitude that if you were there for a year, you were pretty well qualified to hang out your shingle. I myself feel like it's probably more like four or five years in a good shop before I would be brave enough to call myself a saddlemaker with a capital S. And I think you could spend even longer if you were in a situation where you were in a shop and could learn to make your own trees. I don't think that's a real short undertaking.

If there is one thing in particular that made our saddles—not *better* than the others, but if that's the word you want to use—would be the fact that we put a lot of pride in having

142

a tree that fits horses to begin with. It doesn't fit every horse in the world but it fits an ideal horse better than most trees come close to, and it will fit poor horses better as well.

We work with a shop rule that's been cowboy tradition, or would seem to be, that a good saddle was supposed to cost that cowboy three months wages. A cowboy can come in and order not *close* to, but *exactly* what he wants down to the finest detail. They are made to take a hard day's work and be comfortable. We use the finest leather and hardware, and I feel like we are qualified to decorate it however anybody might even dream they'd like a saddle. That in total, combined with the price, makes them a bargain. It's the quality that goes with a proper pricing. For myself, I guess, that's what separates good saddles from bad.

Some people never do lose that striving to make a dollar. Their whole life revolves around how much money they can make. I think that limits how nice a work you can turn out. I'd much sooner earn a dollar an hour making something I'm real pleased with as ten dollars an hour turning out work I'm not pleased with.

Cowboys expect, for their hard-earned dollars, to get a nice piece of work. They wholeheartedly try to become knowledgeable about everything they might come across, and they dang sure appreciate good work. I think cowboys pick up and look at things a lot closer. They want stuff that captures the eye all right, too, but it has to be well made, not just shiny. I don't think there's anything that I can think of that a cowboy uses that is strictly for decoration. Everything has a function. Which is real good because it doesn't let you make artificial stuff. If it doesn't work, it flat doesn't work, no matter how shiny or pretty it is. Pretty soon, you're not a very busy saddle shop.

The grapevine among cowboys is almost as strong as it is amongst saddlemakers. They know everything that goes on everywhere. I think it gets back to the simple fact that they are interested. When a new cowboy is in camp with a different type of gear, they go to asking a lot of questions and finding out about it. Inevitably amongst the questions is "Who made it?" Pretty soon they know about you and the kind of work you do and practically everything about you.

The kind of miles a ranch cowboy puts on a saddle are so long and hard in comparison to say a rodeo cowboy who's got a saddle on a horse maybe half an hour. A lot of faults start to stand out when you put them to that hard a use, whether it's soreing horses, which isn't allowed, or anything.

I think for a cowboy looking at a saddle, he sees farther than just the embellishment on the outside. I think for people downtown, the only thing they pay attention to is what catches their eye. If it's not a decorated saddle, then they might not know good from bad. Whereas a cowboy can look at two roughout saddles and see a lot farther into the two of them than the fellow just standing there that's ignorant to it. I think cowboys are, in particular, more in tune with nice work. They always have been. If you pick up the earliest saddle catalog you can find, it's been ranch, not rodeo or show cowboys, that have supported the nicest old saddle shops, Visalia or whoever. It's tradition and pride. A lot of pride goes into it. They might drive the worst old rattiest pickup and they'll have the nicest looking saddle rolled up in the back that you could ever come across. I guess it's because it's what they spend their life in. He's going to ride the nicest saddle he can afford, but it has to go beyond looks. It has to do what it's supposed to do while he's out there. It seems to be passed on from the old cowboys to the young ones that just riding some saddle isn't good enough. It should be a very nice saddle. It should be a very nice bit. It shouldn't just be something to get you by. You should get something of very good quality because it's something that is supposed to last you a long time and it's supposed to do a certain job.

JEREMIAH WATT, *Saddlemaker and silversmith*
Millarville, Alberta, Canada

I went to work for Mr. J. L. Mercer in 1949 and bought him out in 1959. We're called Mercer Boot Company, which is not to be confused now with J. L. Mercer and Son, who came back into the business nearly thirty years after they'd sold out to me. Mr. Mercer had been in operation since the early twenties. He'd made boots for different bootmakers in and around the area up until he'd put in his business around 1928. I worked for him ten years until I bought him out.

The design on our vamp is called a toe flower. It is always the same pattern on the foot, that's our trademark. Every bootmaker has a design on the vamp. Also, our oak leaf stitch pattern on the tops, which we use practically exclusive is recognized because people see it over and over. We'll make them any way a customer wants, but most of them want them the way we've designed them for years and years and years. They like the design is the reason they buy the boot.

Eugene López is my shop foreman. He's been with me since I bought out Mercer in 1959. I think Mr. López makes the best boots most people have ever seen or worn. I think he's the best bootmaker in the United States. He can do every phase of it from the tops to the finished product. He was trained in Llano, Texas, by Charlie Garrison, another one of the old-time bootmakers that was famous all over the U.S. Garrison taught him and brought him up as a child, and he was later his shop foreman until he died.

Mr. López trains all of our employees. We start them out as an apprentice, part-time. When they learn it, we work them into full-time. Every employee we have is trying to make a boot better than the next person that comes along, even in our own category of hand-made boots. We feel like we make a prettier boot that will look better, fit better and shape to the foot better than other bootmakers'. They don't stay around here very long if they don't take pride in their work.

We make about twenty pair a week right now and about a thousand pair a year. I imagine we have twenty thousand customers on the books. Once we make them a pair or two of boots, they come back year after year—and their children and their children's children. It's just been that way. We've made boots for Texas Governor John Connally and

Lyndon Johnson, for all the celebrities in the country and people all over the United States. But our main source of customers comes from the people that really have to use the boot.

We have more or less the most handmade boot of any boot company in the country. We hand-peg all the shanks. We do our inseam and welts by hand. We use leather toe boxes when a lot of people use a plastic toe box. We put them on the last and let them stay for two weeks to dry where most people run them right on through the same day. We don't have any equipment except sewing machines; we do the rest of it by hand—just a needle and thread. When we put in the welt that you attach the sole to, we put every stitch in there by hand. We wax those strings and when we pull it in there and beat it down, it's not gonna leak. The water is not going to come through and the dust is not going to come through. That's just part of the handmade part that the factory can't do. Theirs'll run over, they don't keep their shape and they don't have the best leather in them. Of course, we use the finest leather that can be had.

A cowboy can get two, three or four years' wear out of our boots where he wouldn't get six months out of what we call a "hand-me-down" boot, or factory boot. A machine can't pull their welts in there as tight, a machine can't pull it over the last as tight. Those things make a nice-looking boot, but they just don't have the quality. They just don't have the strength we can put into a boot.

I take all the measurements when a man wants a pair of boots made. I fit the boot to the last. I used to make the boots, but I don't anymore. I just do the fitting and take the measurements and be sure they get the right fit, which I've had forty-five years' experience doing.

Of course there's not as many cowboys as there used to be. A lot of them use pickups instead of horses now. So many of them don't wear boots to cowboy in like they did in the old days, they wear them for dress. We sell a lot of exotics now like ostrich and alligator and things, strictly for dress. We're making a pair of boots right now for the Texas Sesquicentennial with the Alamo and flag on one side and capital building and the native bird of Texas on the other. People are not using boots today for the purpose they were intended to be used for. We're making a lot of round-toed, flat-heeled boots that look like shoes, they're strictly for comfort. But now, since people don't ride . . . .

We wish it was like it used to be in the old days when we could make them for people who used them in their occupation. Then they would know how good the boots are. In the old days the purpose of the real pointed, square toe—quarter box they called it—was that you could slip your foot in the stirrup much more easily. The higher heel had a purpose too. It would hold your foot in the stirrup, it wouldn't slide through. That's the type of boot we wish we could make everybody, but we have to do whatever is necessary to make a living in this business. It's a shame that it's not the way it used to be, but it just isn't.

WALTER W. WEAVER, *Bootmaker*
Mercer Boot Company
San Angelo, Texas

Gary Dunshee, Saddlemaker, Big Bend Saddlery, Alpine, Texas.

Saddle by Scott Brown, Elko, Nevada. Silver by Mark Dahl, Deeth, Nevada.

We try to cater to the people who really use the equipment. They are the type of people who really appreciate the art, the little extra we try to put into it.

NANCY PETERSON
Three Forks Saddlery
Three Forks, Montana

If it don't ring, it ain't a spur.

GREG LOCKE, *Cowboy*
Padlock Ranch
Hardin, Montana

147

I'm retired. I worked on ranches in California, Arizona, New Mexico, Oregon and Nevada. Spent one winter in Texas and fed some cattle on wheat. Don't miss it too much now, I'm getting too old. I just got a hobby now. I gather up old bits and rawhide stuff and trade. I travel a little, not much. I go to horse doings where I know people, mostly to visit with them. I have a few horses this side of Tecate and I go down and look after them. Pensioner horses, just like me.

I also go visit with them Mexican craftsmen and watch the boys do their work. Old Israel Medina, he stands right over them most of the time when they're making that fancy stuff. He has a pair of reins there that were real small, I think three-eights of an inch. It's thirty-six strands of rawhide. You can't hardly see them, they're so fine. They spent three years making them. No, they're not for sale. He's got some hackamores that are made thirty-two-strand and he wants thirty-two hundred dollars for them. He's really the craftsman. He figures all them things out in his head. He had a rawhide headstall, complete, curb strap and everything made fine out of that and he said, "Sure took a lot of figuring to do it." Old Israel has a lot of pride. He likes to look at them beautiful things. "Beautiful," he says. He knows he's one of the best in it.

Arnulfo Ortiz, he had a job down in Tecate and he was making stuff out of old cow tails and everything, but he finally got it going and then he got to importing mane hair. Now he makes fancy belts and headstalls, lots of hair ropes and puts the buttons on rawhide reins and headstalls and hobbles in horsehair hitching.

Luis Ortega, he's the best. He makes probably the best usable stuff as anybody. These boys can't make riatas. Ortega could make good riatas. The Mexicans on them ranches, now they can make extremely good ones, but these guys that braid them reins, they just don't have the knack of making them riatas. They can't compete with Ortega in them ways. Ortega is retired and doesn't do any of it anymore. This fancy stuff of Israel's is too fancy to use. It's just for show. I wouldn't want to compare them with Ortega. Ortega is the best there has ever been. He doesn't make it as fancy, but he made it to really use. Ortega never *tried* to make it that fancy but he could have if he'd have wanted to, I'm sure. Ortega, probably in his day and probably still, is the king.

I don't really go to sell it. I just go to bumming around here and there and when people that I know want to buy a piece or trade, if I've got something, I'll let them have it. If I make a little bit of my gasoline money, that's all right. If I don't, it's all right. I just like to have it in my home. I like for people to come visit and look at it. I don't make money on it. If I counted my running around, I'd be in the hole.

GEORGE MOORE, *Trader*
Fernley, Nevada

148

Hatband (maker unknown), Chihuahua, Chihuahua, Mexico.

Inlaid saddle tree (maker unknown), Guadalajara, Mexico.

Rawhider Frank Hansen, Lakeview, Oregon, wearing bolo by Luis Ortega, Paradise, California.

Rawhide by Israel Medina, Tecate, Baja, California. Horsehair hitched buttons by Arnulfo Ortiz, Tecate, Baja, California.

Brass oxbow stirrup by Bob Douglas, Sheridan, Wyoming. Engraving by Chip Drusch, Churchill, Montana. Boots by Paul Bond, Nogales, Arizona.

Mr. Werner came to the U.S. as an immigrant in the early 1900s. His uncle put him on a boat when his parents died, and he got a job in Iowa in a harness shop building and repairing harness being used while they were digging the Panama Canal. He worked ten hours a day and lived in a boarding house. He got paid two dollars and fifty cents a week for hand-stitching ten hours a day. It cost him two-fifty a week to live in the boarding house, so he delivered telegrams after work and got a dime a day for his spending money. He worked a while at Miles City Saddlery in Montana and finally wound up in Alpine and bought this saddle shop about 1926.

George Nix went to work for him in '47 and he told me when he'd show up for work about eight o'clock, Mr. Werner had already been there working for about three hours. Then Mr. Werner would go to the Texas Cafe and eat a breakfast steak, three or four eggs and a big old plate of biskits and gravy every morning. He'd come back about nine o'clock and go to drinking beer. He kept about ten cases of beer in the back and he'd drink that beer hot, all day long. He'd stay there until George got back from lunch and then Mr. Werner would go to the Toltec Bar and stay over there until it was time for George to get off. He'd come back to the shop, George would go home, and Mr. Werner would put in about another eight hours that night.

George worked for Mr. Werner two different times and in between went to Phoenix and worked for N. Porter. George bought the shop in 1964 and I bought it from George's widow in 1977 after I'd worked for George six years. I hired on as a stamp hand and he was getting seven dollars and fifty-cents for a full flower-stamped belt then. I got a third. I could stamp about a belt a day, so I was making two-fifty a day until I learned how to speed things up a little and got better at it.

In later years Mr. Werner lived with George and his wife and then was put in a nursing home. I would go to the nursing home and pick him up and take him to the Toltec every afternoon so he could drink beer with his buddies. I was at the shop by myself, so I'd take him down there just before I opened after lunch and I couldn't go back for him until I closed at six o'clock. Boy, he'd be smooth running drunk when I got back over there and I'd just drive him up to that nursing home and turn him out. One day the nurses met me at the door: the night before he'd been chasing all the old women up and down the halls there!

George was always griping at me for being so slow. He said, "By God, I can build two saddles in a week." I'd think, "Now, that's a bunch of bull." I'd be around there and it would take him a month to tie one off. So I asked Mr. Werner one day on the way to the Toltec, "Is it true you can build two saddles in a week?" He kind of perked up and looked at me and said, "Well, yeah, I guess it is. I used to build six a week." But some of his saddles kind of look like it, too.

I did nothing but stamp belts for a year before he'd even let me start *repairing* saddles. Then when I started repairing them, he made me repair everything in the world. I've went through a million different saddles of every kind and description. I think you can learn an awful lot about saddle making from repairing old saddles. You get to see so many different ways people put saddles together and what they did when they built it. That's what I think was valuable, not the actual repairing. I can spot a Donaho or an N. Porter or a Leddy or a Ryon or a Frank Vela a mile off now. I've repaired two or three saddles that wets were riding that were Madison Square Garden Champion Cowboy saddles. Everything you can imagine from old sorry cheesecloth-covered trees to the good ones.

The only thing I'm sorry I never got to see was any of the northern-type saddles. I don't think I ever even saw one until five years ago. I've got a lot of admiration for the way they build things up there. I think their entire saddle-making process had a different beginning from ours. I could take the saddle I built before I went up there and the saddle I built whenever I got back and it would be like black and white. I think the style saddle you use is whatever you need for your country, your horses and yourself. But their craftsmanship is above and beyond anything you'll see in Texas. They put more heart into it. They're more interested in the person and the horse that's getting it than they are in what they're getting for it. I think that's the way it ought to be.

The guys I've been around in the past five years also seem to be a lot more interested in their gear, their horses and how they do their job. They put a little more heart into their job, just like the saddle makers, instead of just get it done so they can make a buck and go on. It kind of sends cold chills up my back when somebody that knew George or Mr. Werner comes in and pats me on the back and says, "You learned real good, you build a saddle just like George." I like to think that mine are a little *different*.

GARY DUNSHEE, *Saddlemaker*
Big Bend Saddlery
Alpine, Texas

152 *Overlay and bit by Phillip Osborn, Maljamar, New Mexico.*

Bosal (on bay horse) by Bill Black, MC Ranch, Adel, Oregon; mecate by Blind Bob Mills, Kettleman City, California. Bosal (on gray horse) by Jack Sheppard, Payette, Idaho; mecate by Larry Schutte, Maggie Creek Ranch, Carlin, Nevada.

Bit and headstall by Jeremiah Watt, Millarville, Alberta, Canada.

Bit by Bill Klapper, Pampa, Texas.

Forged knives by Lee Reeves, Gage, Oklahoma.

I like to make a knife people will use. A big knife tends to spend more time hanging on the wall or laying in a drawer somewhere. If a knife gets too bulky, you won't carry it. I also don't like a pocket knife because when I want to get it out, I'm usually in a position where I've got to stop what I'm doing, stand up and dig around in my pocket.

Once I got into mild steel forging, I went from simple punches and shoes deeper and deeper into metalurgy, learning the way heat affects steel. Heating and hammering a knife realigns the grains in the steel and packs them. I think you get a tougher knife than you would by the stock removal method. Of course forging is complicated and you can also forge flaws into a knife if you don't know what you are doing.

Back in the Middle Ages, knifesmiths fostered the idea that they used the elements: fire, iron and air—and did something magical to the iron to make it steel. They kept their techniques secret and claimed supernatural powers for their knives. That aura still persists. A lot of this is just knowing how the steel feels under the hammer, and its color. The light in your shop affects the color, so you have to experiment or use a pyrometer until you know how they show up in your particular light. You have to temper the steel, hold it at a low heat, to relieve the inner tension enough to give it toughness. Tempering is a trade-off between hardness and toughness. You want it hard enough to keep an edge, but tough enough so it won't break when you are trying to use it.

You can't really tell by looking that my knives are hand-forged. I've made some knives where I've left a few rough spots on purpose right in front of the guard. But the steel I use isn't stainless and they take a little care to keep them rust-free. Any rough spot will collect dirt and rust them more easily. So I generally take all the forge marks out. Some of these high-alloy stainless steel knives are almost impossible to sharpen. You have to wait until you get back to an electric grinder to sharpen them. I try to temper the knife I make where it will hold an edge well, but you can sharpen it on a pocket stone.

I don't think I would want to be a full-time knife maker. A professional knife maker will have a whole batch of knives going at once, but I like to concentrate on one at a time. I think a lot of the fun would go out of it if I had to make them for a living. I think that in general, people have gotten tired of the mass-produced anything. When things were handmade there were only a few, and those few were very good. There is a mystique to something handmade, particularly to a handmade knife. A knife is such an elemental tool, a primal tool. It is so simple, and yet it's been around so long.

LEE REEVES, *Horseshoer*
Gage, Oklahoma

One of the things I like to hear them say is, "I want it whenever you can get it." You can't rush an artist.

CHIP DRUSCH, *Silversmith*
Churchill, Montana

I feel a little bit of hand touch improves the quality. Quality is the most important thing in any given piece. Everyone should aim for the best quality at any price. I want to be the best.

FRANCISCO CORTES II, *Silversmith*
Cortes Joyeros
Guadalajara, Jalisco, Mexico

Boots by Walter W. Weaver and Eugene Lopez, Mercer Boot Company, San Angelo, Texas. Spurs by Steve Fredieu, Fort Worth, Texas.

Badger skin packers by Bill Stuart, Desert Leather Company, Carson City, Nevada.

My extra time is devoted to napping, making hair McCartys, rawhiding, colts and family. Back when I started making them, you couldn't afford the price of a nice, usable hair rope on buckaroo wages. I was around Bill Kane at Tuscarora who was making ropes, and I picked up how to make them. A good rope is like any piece of art. An artist, when he's building something, is going to have a fit every time. He'll find a flaw in his work. So you just keep building on that, what you can do better, what implements you can use to make a better rope next time. Same with boot making, rawhiding, making horses, you're always going to try to be better at it.

There's a definite way of building them strings. It's the way that hair is laid out so your string don't have a lot of hair sticking out of it. There's very few people making them kind of string where they're smooth. Bill Kane makes a good string and Blind Bob. When you go to looking for good ropes, they're priced up there too, but there's a lot of time put into the preparation of that string. The ideal way to make them strings is with each individual hair pointed with the root end going one way, so when you feed that string, that root is in the inside of the string. Then you get it to laying down. There's no hair sticking up, no curlicues or twists. Then in the twist itself, when you're putting that rope together, the evenness of how that rope is going together is another indication of a good rope. I make a four-string rope right now. There's no core in it. I just put the extra hair in the string. That makes that string last longer. The smaller the string, like in rawhiding, it's more liable to wear. With a larger string, you can use less of them. You still have the smoothness and prettiness, but it just lasts a little longer.

The Spanish talked about different tightness of ropes and different hair, like coarse hair. It's the same as with a coarser or stiffer bosal. If the horse's head was a little bit heavy, they had to use that to lighten his face up. The hair was the same thing: when it comes up on the bars of his chin, he'll get away from it a little quicker. Then as they softened up, you went either to a softer bosal or smoother McCarty with mane hair. Some horses are so sensitive you have to use human hair. But that depends on the hands too.

I like ropes that I don't have to pick up. A real soft rope, you have to pick the whole thing up. One that's pretty tight, that's not stiff, but where there's plenty of life in it, you can just pick it up with your little finger. Besides tradition, a hair rope has a better feel to it. You can buy these store-bought McCartys, nylon and that, and some people like them. Some people only use hair ropes when they go to town. But there's a better feel to a hair rope. Myself, say you're roping, dragging calves, I notice that hair will take the sweat out of my palms and I can keep a hold of it better. Store-bought stuff is slick until it's drug through the sweat and the mud and the dirt, then it gets rough. Hair McCartys, you can get different colors and different life in them. Store-bought stuff is just there. When it's new it's soft, when it's dirty, it's stiff.

LARRY SCHUTTE, *Buckaroo*
Maggie Creek Ranch
Carlin, Nevada

Sherry Dugan, Nye, Montana.

CHAPTER SIX

THE WOMEN

The ladies beside, behind—
or in the lead

I'M ONE OF TODAY'S WOMEN whose life is still linked to the way of the cowboy, but I'm not quite sure which one I am. Some days I want to be Cindy Goddard, who can do anything a man can do, and other days I want to be Lucille Moorhouse and hang up curtains and make a good country home for my family.

My first experience with Cowgirls' Lib came back during my young single days in Arizona. I was helping at a producers' feed yards and the foreman assigned me to ride pens with a dashing young cowboy. The cowboy looked me up and down, looked the boss in the eye and said, "I'll be glad to go to bed with her but I ain't ridin' with no woman." Needless to say, he got neither opportunity.

Since marrying a cowboy, I've lived under almost every edict, from helping every day to being forbidden to even show up, and I'm still not sure which way I want it. I've seen marriages go on the rocks because the wife couldn't ride and I've seen them go on the rocks when a new woman was hired to work with a bunch of men. Everybody is human and heartstrings are hard to control.

I've also known very few women, maybe only two, who could do a cowboy's job completely. Usually a man shod their horses, roped the rankest stock, rode the toughest horses, took the roughest trails and pointed the yearlings. Just to "go along" takes needed horses out of the remuda and puts a bigger burden on some man or men, not to mention complicating the logistics of bathing and answering nature's call. Some men handle the inconvenience better than others, and so do some women.

Cowboys' wives seemed to be more content back when there were fewer modern conveniences and they had a "real job" just taking care of necessities like gardening, canning

159

and washing. But times have changed, and it's harder today for a cowboy's wife to find fulfillment in her side of the partnership. She needs to feel useful. My friend Susan Stephens says, "The biggest thing about me riding these horses is that it gives me something to do. It gives me a feeling of self-worth, accomplishment."

My husband says a horse needs a real job before he can be a happy horse. I think the same goes for cowboys' wives. The tough part is finding a real job. I still don't know what I want to be when I grow up.

How much you can take a cow before she gets hot and wants to get on the fight just depends on your judgment. Or the same with a horse or your dog—how much pressure you can put on him before he'll quit you or gets too hot. Those things just take living before you can figure them out. Yeah, and on my wife. I know where the pressure point is on her!

My wife's helped me start a lot of horses. She can't rope as good as I can, quite. Not that I'm a good roper—and she does fine, too. But she just hasn't roped as much as I have. She's a natural at cowboying or handling cows, just natural. I've known guys that cowboyed a lot that couldn't do half what she can. But starting them horses, we catch them by the hind foot. I let her do the roping and then I do the saddling and riding. I get so frustrated because she takes shots that Monty Montana couldn't make and then here's a perfect setup and she doesn't shoot for it. So I'm around there, "Okay, get ready, shoot! Aw, no! Now, you see, when he was like that, you can shoot, see?" Pretty soon I got her so wound up, she's wanting to go to the house. So I could see that wasn't working. I just had to learn to keep my mouth shut. But it's so difficult because I want her to be where I am and that's tough. She just has to have more living, more roping. Finally, I got to where I'd say, "Catch this guy by the hind foot here. I got to get something at the barn. I'll be back in a minute." And I'll go to the barn and peek through a knothole. When she's got him caught, then I come back out.

I've mellowed out in my old age. When she first knew me, I was quite a bit wilder than what I am now. And she has flat quit me if I lose my temper working over a dog or a cow or a horse. So I got so I knew where she was liable to quit me and I didn't let myself get there. I'd lose her and I was needing her for help. I had a real good dog one time and you could get mad and start hollering at a cow. The dog was so sensitive, good little dog, he'd just flat quit me. Then I felt like a fool because I'd let myself get that far. I thought, "Good for you, I needed quitting." My wife's been good for me, too. I wouldn't want her to take some of that immature crap that I was putting out.

BRYAN NEUBERT, *Buckaroo*
Robert R. Marvel Ranches
Lamoille, Nevada

Cindy Goddard, Nye, Montana.

I had had enough of blind dates, especially the kind your own mother arranged. I was tired. I almost didn't agree to go. But I vividly remember opening my front door and there, on my front porch, stood the Marlboro Man in his hat and boots. I knew I was in trouble.

LEE ALLEN, *Rancher's wife*
Allen Ranch
Ozona, Texas

Sometimes I wish Dad had never raised me as a boy, that every time he would get me up at six in the morning, saddle my horse and boost me up to help move cows, Mom would have instead made me stay home and play with my dolls and toy electric stove. Gary Morton said, "Once cowboying is in your blood, it's there to stay." It's just too bad cowboys and cowgirls both have the same red blood, isn't it?

SONYA GODDARD, *Cowgirl*
Dodge City, Kansas

Chris had a very deep, personal love for the land and the ranch. I couldn't understand how he could feel so strongly about this place and this kind of life. He expects a lot. He wanted me to do everything and do it well. I felt like wearing a big sign around my neck that said to the cowboys, "I'm here not because I want to invade all of your privacy. Chris told me to do this." I always tried to keep a low profile.

It was a hard time. He wanted me but everybody else didn't want me. When Chris had a lesson he wanted to get across to the men, if he was mad or had a complaint about something, he usually used me to take it out on, in front of everybody. That way the men got the point, but he didn't yell at them. I never slept. And for a long time when he first had me go on roundups, he completely ignored me. I guess he didn't want to show any favoritism. I don't know why I love it so much. I know what he means, now.

I learned the secret of life. You're out there and you wake up early in the morning and go to the chuck wagon. You eat breakfast and they bring in the remuda and everybody starts to rope out their horses. You're standing there and you get this chill. Something unique is about to happen and I am privileged enough to be part of it. You don't want to do anything to wake up from this dream. I'm almost desperate with hope that won't happen.

DIANE LACY, *Rancher's wife*
o6 Ranch
Fort Davis, Texas

Colleen and Jeremiah Watt, Millarville, Alberta, Canada.

We lived at the Bell Ranch headquarters and at three different camps before Gary became wagon boss and we moved back to headquarters. When Gary and I worked together most was at the Mosquero Camp on the Bell's. I couldn't help every day because I had the girls, but when somebody couldn't come to help him, I helped him. When they hire one man on a ranch—they get two. But, except of course for the owner's daughter, no women were allowed to go with the crew. I resented the hell out of the fact that the women couldn't go along. I could respect their attitudes, but I still resented it at the same time. Which has nothing to do with women's lib. It's a life style, not a job. And you love it as much as they do, but you can't partake in it because of the "Code of the West." I knew it wasn't Gary's fault. No matter what we've ever done, Gary and I were partners. But when you hire onto an outfit, you have to play by their rules if you plan to stay there—if you like it well enough. I think it's a problem within the men themselves. That's why I admire Gary so much: because he sees me, or any other woman, as another human being.

SUZIE MORTON, *Cowboy's wife*
Lincoln, New Mexico

163

Sharon Burcham, Sand Creek Ranch, Big Sandy, Montana.

I grew up on a family ranch in Idaho. My family are Basque. We had sheep and then later cattle; we were horseback all the time. We had a place in the valley and we trailed in the spring to the summer range and then trailed out in the fall.

Dean and I lived at the IL for a year. I was a cook. They had a wagon and the women weren't allowed at the wagon. So when the wagon went out with the cows, the men went and we'd see our husbands just once in a while. I think that's kind of silly. They didn't even like us to go out there and *visit* if they were close by. I think that's really silly. I think if they're a family, they ought to allow for things like that. I didn't like it. Tradition, I guess. That's the way it used to be, that's the way it should be or they *think* it should be now. That's the way the old timers did it. The women were at home and the men followed the cattle around. But we're together now. We've got a little house called Eighteen Mile. If he rides any, I can help him. I can ride with him.

I grew up on a ranch and I've had horses all my life and been around stock all my life, but I had brothers, see. The brothers got to do everything. *We* got to *cook.* So I know a little bit about a horse and a little bit about a cow. But as far as what you'd call a cowboy or a

164

cowgirl—I guess I know as much as some but not as much as a lot of them. There's a lot of talent there that I never learned because we were in the kitchen. At all the brandings, where you had opportunities like that, we were in the kitchen until the dishes were done. I'm not going to hold my daughter back that way. She's really horse-minded and I want her to be able to do what she wants to do. She can always learn to cook.

Dean and I started twenty-one head of horses a few years back and we started draft horses. We went in a sheep wagon from Paradise Valley to the IL, and I drove the team and pulled the wagon and he came along with the horses or the cavvy. We like that. In fact, that's what we're looking for: a little place where we can work together. Have a few draft horses, hay with the draft horses and just work as a team.

One time I had a side-delivery rake and Dean was on the rake with me, teaching me along. We were working some mules named Tom and Jerry. He let me go on my own and the first thing I did on my first turn was turn too sharp into the rake. The back of one mule hit the rake and we had a runaway. You're in a man's world out there and the first thing you do is mess up, it seems like. That's tough right off, to be out there with the men and have to compete with them and their knowledge and skill. But you just do the best you can.

Dean is really patient and understanding. Like starting those horses, and starting the way he does, on the ground. We laid all the horses down. That was fun. That was a new experience for me. Any time you can learn like that, it's good. I feel like I can go out and hay, and I'm good with animals. It's not like I'm the dummy that doesn't know how to do anything. I know what to do and what not to do, most of the time. You have the opportunity on a ranch to share that type of life. It's not like either one of you is going to a nine-to-five job somewhere in the city where you can't share. When you get on a place and you can't, that's sad.

REVA TOBIAS, *Buckaroo's wife*
Gamble Ranch
Montello, Nevada

Nobody bends over backwards, but I think all of the men are conscious that the women need to be treated with the same respect you'd give to another cowboy. It's tough being a lady. You have to work harder. You say things to your wife—tell her she ought to be over here, move faster—things you'd never say to another man. Bill rode up the other day and asked me why we do that.

RON GODDARD, *Cowboy*
Penokee, Kansas

WAGON WIDOW

I was thinkin' just the other day 'bout the names that people dream up,
So peculiar to a region or the kind of work they're in.
The Pacific Northwest lumber camps have men they call the whistle punks,
And the steeplejack has courage and the eagle is his friend.

And the men who sail the oceans have a language of their own,
And the men who dig the coal out of the mines.
And the men out in the West who ride the range and work the cattle
Have a name for someone special on their minds.

She's called a wagon widow, but her husband he ain't dead yet,
It just seems to her he's hardly ever home.
He's out brandin' calves or shippin' steers or maybe movin' yearlin's,
And he sleeps out at the wagon and she has to stay alone.

And it ain't that he don't love her or want to have her with him,
It's just hard to break tradition, hard to open up our minds.
So that ranch-raised girl who loves to ride the range and work the cattle
Is a wagon widow during roundup time.

When the widows get together for an evening on the town,
They pretend they're having fun and things are fine.
Then they drive back to the ranch and pray the brandin' don't get rained on,
That the roundup goes on schedule this time.

And the widow keeps the chores done up and checks the calvy heifers,
And does the jobs the cowboys do with only half the time.
Tho' she feels a bit neglected, she gets stronger every roundup,
And her pistol's on the nightstand when she goes to bed at night.

When roundup time is over and things are back in order,
And there's autumn leaves mixed in among the pines,
They can saddle up together and ride out side by side,
And the widow once again becomes a bride.

And the men who sail the oceans have a language of their own,
And the men who dig the coal out of the mines.
And the men out in the West who ride the range and work the cattle
Have a name for someone special on their minds.

JOEL NELSON, *Cowboy*
o6 Ranch
Alpine, Texas

Pat Jordan, Bozeman, Montana.

Mom used to pack us in a salt pannier when we were about a month old. That sounds cruel doesn't it? I started riding when I was about three and Dad started us breaking colts when we were six. We all helped him ride and brand and break colts, and he taught us to rope when we were real young.

Greg used to tell me when I helped him that he didn't approve of women riding. When we got married, I told him that I rode and that's all I knew because that's how I was raised. I figured if he didn't like it, he'd get used to it. I just ignored him and rode anyway. I proved to him that I could do just about what he could do.

There are some horses Greg won't let me ride. A lot of times I'll just snub for him. That used to bother me but now I kind of feel that he doesn't want me to get out there and get hurt. If a bull gets on the fight real bad, I get a little antsy. I'll rope a cow but I won't rope a bull. I'll let Greg handle that. It bothers me sometimes. I sit there and think, I'm out here trying to help them and when a bull gets on the fight and they really need me to help, I can't, really. I'll heel one for them, but I won't head them. It bothers me that I can't be more help when a situation like that comes up.

We went to work on a big outfit in Texas and they didn't allow me to ride, even when we had a camp. If they saw me out riding with Greg, they used to get pretty upset. Especially if I was riding one of the ranch horses. They never gave us any reason, just said it was an old ranch and women never rode on that place. They just thought a girl should stay home and cook for all the men. They thought girls didn't know anything. They wouldn't give me a chance to prove myself; they didn't allow that. Most of the other wives either didn't like to ride or they had kids in school and just never rode. I talked to the men about it and they said it didn't bother them. But the older men who had been there a long time didn't approve. At first Greg thought it was all right, he thought I should stay home. It caused a lot of trouble between us. We had a camp, just me and him, but they didn't want me helping him outside the house. After a while, Greg thought it was pretty unfair too.

The Chilicote Ranch is the only ranch that ever paid me. No one minds there, they kind of expected me to help them. At first they just said I could ride, but when I started helping every day, they decided they'd start paying me day wages. When they got the crew together to start branding, I got my own string of horses and no one else was allowed to ride them but me. My dad always taught me it was all right for women to ride. But on a big crew—it's all right for women to come out to the wagon but not to stay in camp. I guess that's just old-fashioned bringing up. I've asked a lot of people and they've always just said that's the way it's always been. They've never really given me a reason why not. A lot of people say women get in the way, and I'm sure some women do. But I know a lot of men that get in the way too!

FRAN LOCKE, *Cowboy's wife*
Padlock Ranch
Hardin, Montana

Kathleen and Ron Goddard, Mountain Island Ranch, Glade Park, Colorado.

No, my wife doesn't get to ride as much as she used to. We've got two little boys now and they pretty well keep her tied down. It's a pretty big change for her because she never . . . even growing up she was with her dad a lot on these ranches, and riding. When I married her she could hardly cook. She'll tell you that. She was kind of a tomboy. She used to ride with me before we had these kids, but she's real sensitive and she's pretty careful about who she gets around. But if she's around friends and family she likes to get horseback, and she's good help, too. I hope when the boys get old enough to go with us, that she will ride again.

MARTIN BLACK, *Buckaroo*
Gamble Ranch
Montello, Nevada

169

When it's just Larry and I, I help him at our end of the ranch. But when the whole crew comes, I don't go. They don't say anything, but it's my choice. I feel uncomfortable around all those guys, me being the only girl. If there was other women around, I'd go more often. Why do I feel that way? 'Cause I'm not a women's libber. A lady should be a lady. But if she needs to get out there and help, then she should be out there helping. When there's a bunch of guys around and they can do the job, there's no sense in me being out there. Except for when they brand and I like to rope, so I'm there then whether they want me there or not!

I'm a licensed cosmetologist in Idaho and Nevada, so if anything ever happened to Larry, I could go back to work. But not that I want to. I do a lot of artwork in all mediums: oils, pen-and-inks, watercolors, pencil—a little bit of everything. And I'm starting to do some sculptures. It's an outlet for me. When I do my artwork, it's like I'm in a whole other world. The whole world could crash down around me and I'd never know. It's just something I like to do, it's relaxing. There is definitely not the time, you just have to make it if you want to do it.

I can tie rawhide buttons, I can braid, I do horsehair hitching. I do everything from cooking for the crew to helping them brand, teach the kids, help ride, fix fence, just everything. This summer, I ran the swather for the hay crew. I hadn't done that for about fifteen years. I thought, "Boy, I'm getting old. I can't do this stuff!" But it didn't take me long and I was out there doing it again. I don't do anything very well, but, I can do a lot of things. Sometimes I think I should just stick with one thing, like my art or the braiding, and be good at it. But I need the variety.

I got in the Jordan Valley Big Loop Rodeo this year for the first time. It was quite an experience, quite an honor, especially being a woman. The best thing was that my husband asked me if I'd rope with him, so that was even better yet. The Big Loop is a horse roping. You head and front-foot a colt. Your loop has to be twenty foot around, ten foot in one direction. You come out of a barrier kind of like team roping. It's a timed event, romantic event. I did the front-footing. I tried to head too, because Larry missed, but I front-foot. I got in another horse roping with Ross Knox quite a few years ago and we did a lot of practicing. But when it came right down to the show and the tension and everything, well, it wasn't very good. But I enjoy that.

I was raised in the country and have lived on a ranch all my life. I like my privacy. I like being by ourselves. It's just a neat way of living. I can't say it's any better than anything else, because I don't know what it's like to live in town. For myself, I don't feel like I have to give up anything. But the kids, they can't do all the things the town kids get to do. When I was growing up, we only lived thirty miles out of town. We were still close enough and lived in a large enough community where there was a lot of activities: 4-H, being able to come to

170

Victoria Zermeno, Rancho de Corazon, Guadalajara, Jalisco, Mexico.

town and go swimming, and doing a lot of things the town kids get to do. Now, we're farther out and the kids don't have that advantage. They do miss out on the swimming lessons and the music lessons and the 4-H and all of that. Hopefully, someday we might move to a place where we're still out, and yet close enough that the kids can do that. I miss that for them.

But I think there are a lot of advantages for the kids too. They're fishing, they're riding, they've got their chores to do. When it's time to move cows, they've got their own horses. We need their help. I feel like that's important—knowing that you're needed. I can hear myself saying one word over and over, that I really dislike: "I." I, Toni, can do nothing. Whatever I am or do, it is all by the grace of God, from buckaroo and artist to housewife and mother.

TONI SCHUTTE, *Buckaroo's wife*
Maggie Creek Ranch
Carlin, Nevada

Laura and Ty Holland, JD Ranch, Kent, Texas.

I always lived in town. The hardest thing for me to adjust to at first was not having people around all the time. Now that's the thing that I really enjoy. There's a certain amount of adjustment every woman has to make to become a wife, anyway, and you just have to learn to live with that other person. I think a city gal can do it just as easy as a country gal can. The telephone, the electricity and the running water are all things you have to learn to be prepared to be without—either all three at the same time or one at a time. That's part of country life.

I think that support, whether it is moral support or whatever, is the most important contribution a wife can make. If nothing else you can always be the one that stands in the gate and he runs a whole herd of cattle at you and he says, "Get the black one!" And there's *four* black ones in there. You can always be somebody to holler at and blame because the wrong black one got out.

Usually when we go feed, I drive and he's in the back pouring out feed. Well, this last winter it was pretty cold and he'd been out feeding for so long. He feeds in a wagon, a lot of times too with a team, but this particular time we were in the pickup. He said, "You get out and dump the feed out and I'll drive, because I'm really cold. I want to relax for a minute." So I got in the back. He's always fussing at me because I have thrown him out of the back of the pickup a time or two, running over stumps or going a little faster than I should. He's always fussing and telling me to be careful. Guess who got thrown out of the back of the pickup? I still haven't figured out yet whether it was intentional or not.

KAREN PATTERSON, *Cowboy's wife*
Benjamin, Texas

I think Tom appreciates the fact that I will go with him and that I'm interested and that he can talk to me about the business. I'm a sounding board, sort of. If he can express what he has on his mind, even if I don't give him a good suggestion, he might figure out something to do just from saying it out loud. And he appreciates the fact that I can stay out here and not have to run to town a lot or be lonesome or cause trouble in that way.

Another thing I do, I do keep the cattle count. When we get yearlings in and they're moving them to different fields and everything, it's a pretty good chore to keep up with how many they put where and how many cows are in what pasture and how many calves are branded. So I try to keep up a pretty close count on that. He just appreciates it all and we're good friends and good partners.

It's twenty miles to town to get groceries. If you do any shopping, it's a hundred miles to get to a town big enough to shop. I guess that's kind of a hardship but it probably keeps me from spending too much money. I have to get it all planned out when I go to town: what

I'm going to get, what I need. I know if I had a chance to go to town everyday and see what's for sale, I'd probably buy a lot more than I needed anyway.

When I first saw Tom I thought he was pretty comical looking. He wore a big hat, always overdid his hat. Wore a little red corduroy vest and his pants tucked in his boots. I wasn't really used to all that. But we enjoyed studying together and became good friends and it just went right on. He's grown up now and developed a really good character. He's ambitious but not in a monetary way. He wants to better himself personally, and anything he does, he wants to do it well and in what he feels is the right way. He doesn't want to make more money than anybody else, he just wants to be satisfied with what he's doing and have the satisfaction of knowing he did it his best. He's honest and fair. He's real generous, which a lot of people don't realize because he's also real thrifty. He's a good Christian. Of course, when we married I didn't know all of this. I knew he was a good person but you don't know all those really good qualities about people when you're first around them.

SUE MOORHOUSE, *Rancher's wife*
Moorhouse Ranch Company
Benjamin, Texas

The ranch hand decided to move to Alabama, and that left us with nobody out there to feed the cattle. Ed was about sixteen months old, so we took our baby and moved out to that old ranch house. We took some pots and pans and sheets and bedding and just camped for two or three months. The snow would come and everything would look like a fairyland and the baby and I would go feed the cattle with Togo. We'd come home and cook dinner on that old wood stove.

Then when spring came and it was time to sell the cattle, we just decided it was nice out there, so we'd just stay. They bought more cattle and wintertime came and we built up fires in the fireplace and more fires in that old cookstove. And meantime I'd brought out curtains and little throw rugs and little vases for wildflowers and things that made it look like home, and we just stayed out there. The next year we stayed, and for twenty-five years we stayed and three more sons were born.

We had ambitions, Togo and I did, when we moved out there. First we wanted to raise those little boys good: Christian men. We wanted to educate them and we wanted to pay for the ranch. And we feel like we accomplished all those goals.

LUCILLE MOORHOUSE, *Rancher's wife*
Moorhouse Ranch Company
Benjamin, Texas

Fran and Greg Locke, Padlock Ranch, Hardin, Montana.

Linda Jones, Sierra Vista, Arizona.

I was raised in Arlington, Texas—just a rock-'n'-roll city kid. I was on the annual staff in high school, and I had to take pictures of the guys in FFA with their steers. Oh, I really teased them! They wore boots and I thought they were such hicks. I think it is just poetic justice that I would marry a cowboy.

Right after Jerry and I married, we went to work on the IL Ranch in Tuscarora, Nevada. I cooked for the crew when they were at our camp and sometimes I helped out if the cook was gone or they were between cooks. Our camp was called the Desert Ranch. It was twenty miles from headquarters and the headquarters was eighty-five miles north of Elko. I had never ridden very much and there wasn't much I could have done but get in the way. I went horseback with Jerry about half a dozen times when he was just working around the camp. I really loved it! I heard Jerry talk about "dinks" and I wanted so much not to be in the way and just be a dink.

At the Winecup Ranch in Thousand Springs, Nevada, when I first started going, I didn't ride very well and I was nervous about being horseback. When they'd drop me off on my ride, as soon as I got out of sight, I'd get scared and think the horse was going to run away with me and I'd get hung up and be drug along in the stirrup, but I really wanted to make a hand. Starting from zero, I think I learned a lot. Jerry used to try to drill into me all the etiquette: you don't ride in front of somebody or make them wait for you at a gate, don't get ahead or too far behind and all that. I didn't want to embarrass myself or him whenever we rode. He'd tell me, "Now in this situation you do this, and in this situation you do that." It seemed like I was always misjudging which situation I was in at any time. I'd be thinking, "Now is this one of those situations where I should go help the guy or stay here and do my job?" Meanwhile, the moment passed and it was too late. I'd be riding along concentrating so hard on all the things I was supposed to remember that I wouldn't even notice that half the cattle had turned back on me. Jerry would say, "You just need to wake up a little." When you've met these people and you're so impressed with what they can do, you don't want to be some dink, just riding along behind your husband all day so that you won't get lost or in the way. Sometimes Jerry would critique me in a saccharine-sweet voice and I'd get mad because I thought he was being patronizing. And I'd get mad if he rode a quarter of a mile just to yell at me. It's like your father trying to teach you how to drive. I always wished I could just go work somewhere where nobody knew me—it would have been different.

That was the most beautiful ranch. It was a kick to just be out there. When I was four or five months pregnant with Charlie, I got bucked off and broke my elbow. I had to quit then and since the boys have been born, I really haven't had a chance to ride. I'm anxious to get started again, even if I could just help when they were branding.

There are ladies in Nevada who everyone agrees are really handy and could hold their own with anybody. I think there have always been women who have been good hands. Della Van Norman is a really good hand and made some great horses. The DeLong sisters and Fillis Takacs grew up doing everything on a ranch and they're excellent horsemen. Katy Hertel was a pottery student who came to Tuscarora from California. She liked Tuscarora and Nevada and buckarooing and went to work on a big, dry desert ranch in southern Nevada. She learned every bit of it the hard way and from scratch. She worked right along with the guys, and they put in some long days. When she came back, she'd earned the respect of all the guys she'd worked with.

DEBBIE PARDUE, *Cowboy's wife*
Currycomb Ranch
Carlsbad, New Mexico

What I like to do mostly with my time is ride outside horses. I like to keep two, not more than three, because then things get sort of unbalanced. I can't get my house chores done and Mike gripes at me, justifiably so.

I halter-broke twelve yearling colts for a man that lives south of here. The halter-breaking job just kind of got by him, so they were half grown. That was quite a chore. The first day was real hard on those colts and it was hard on me, too. But I enjoyed it. They were doing pretty good when I sent them home. I was pleased with some but wish I'd have had a little more time with others. I also day-work some for a fellow that lives close by. Some people seem to think if you don't whip up and ride and take over somebody else's territory, you're not a good hand. But I'm gonna do what I think is right whether they think I'm a good hand or not. The extra money sure does come in handy, but the money isn't the biggest thing.

The biggest thing about me riding these horses is that it gives me something to do. It gives me a feeling of self-worth, accomplishment. Before I started riding them, I was sitting around the house, twiddling my thumbs with a pile of housework around me—unhappy. There just wasn't anything that was totally mine. The house is just not what I call a fulfilling life. So the horses and day-work has really been a blessing to me.

If you got a good husband, they're going to help you how and when they can. But I've got to watch myself sometimes because I do take advantage of that and it's not fair of me. Mike's so good about helping me. I've heard lots of women today say they are completely happy tending to their families and doing all the domestic things. A lot of them are afraid of horses. And, gee, whatever it takes to make a person happy—but that's not my thing.

Working cattle was all new to me when we married. I sure enough did feel left out and lonesome. I could ride when we married, so naturally I felt like I needed to be out there. I thought, "This is the pits, this kitchen work." It wasn't like I couldn't ride a horse and couldn't keep up. I knew I could keep up. There wasn't any question about it. But these horses and the little bit of daywork I get to do, that's what I need. It gives me a feeling of self-worth and that's a whole bunch. Of course, I always try to keep my marriage in perspective. Our relationship is my first concern, not the house, but our relationship.

SUSAN STEPHENS, *Cowboy's wife*
Gail, Texas

I haven't been getting to ride near as much as I had hoped to. Mothering does take up some time—but I must say, it's time well spent.

CRILL ALLEN, *Cowboy's wife*
Lovington, New Mexico

Winnie Latta, West Wind Ranch, Gustine, California.

FEBRUARY 22, 1985

Tom and I gathered some bulls yesterday. Had eight old ones we wanted to sell. I'm not real brave workin' them boogers. They also-by-God-lately insist on fighting. They play kind of rough and I darn sure don't want me and my horse in the midst. I always kind of hang back like a borrowed dog.

I'm waitin' for the day when the ranch is paid for and we have some darn good workin' corrals, good fences all around and a log house on the river. I hate where we live now, close to the gravel road and close to neighbors. I would love to live in the middle of nowhere. I also hate having to cobble things up to get by and put up with things that don't work, but economics demands it. Maybe someday.

Stayed in this afternoon and baked bread and caught up with the washing. I count myself lucky when I get half a day inside. Sure would hate to have to stay in full-time, but do appreciate a day once in a while. So far, in thirteen and a half years, I haven't bought a loaf of bread, but sometimes it's a hassle findin' time to bake.

MARCH 3, 1985

We fell off the face of the earth for a couple months. Boy, every year we wonder why we do it. Things around here are pretty darn tired and grouchy and it doesn't take much to make either of us paint for war. We are about done calving heifers tho' so maybe things will get some better. We are down to nine heifers outta a hundred and five, so won't be long till we can sleep all night again. We had a lot of luck calvin' but it was all bad! Seems it was one thing or another. Had to pull a bunch of 'em. Had a smaller set of heifers this year and we were afeared of it. But like Tom says, "This time next year, we will have forgot about it." Is awfully discouraging tho'.

We got socked with a heck of a spring storm the first week or two of calving. We had a foot of snow and a forty-mile-an-hour wind. We had the sheds popping full, but managed to hold the younguns in until it blew over. Sure makes for a mess and lots of extra work.

We have done nothing nor gone anywhere since Februrary. We take turns going out at night, me one night and Tom the next. Some nights we were both up and got very little sleep as we checked at ten P.M., three A.M., and up at five A.M. and then run all day to take care of stock and chores. Not real good on the attitude. I think the kids probably take the brunt of it, tho'.

AUGUST 13, 1985

Has been a real miserable, dry, scary summer here with almost no rain or moisture since that March snowstorm. The pastures never even greened up, and there was virtually no hay on the dryland. Last year we had 120 haybuster stacks off the dry. This year, with

Diane Lacy, 06 Ranch, Alpine, Texas.

oats, hay and all, we've eighteen. That means we'll have to sell all our steer calves, our replacement heifers, and probably 200 out of the 500 cows. Just the shot in the arm we need. So many people, like us, are goin' to be in trouble.

We have been wranglin' cattle from one place to the other tryin' to get by, but come fall most of our winter pasture will be gone.

Tom 'bout has his little ole legs run in the ground, has never seen a summer like this and he too will be glad to see it over. He got a piece of steel in his eye and pert-near went blind 'fore I got him to go into Doc's—went a whole month. Sure do hope his heart is good cuz he'd probably have to have a heart attack 'fore he'd go to town. He claims we have a "stress test" most every day and I'm sure he's right.

JO CASTEEL, *Rancher's wife*
TC Outfit
Vale, South Dakota

Lee Allen, Allen Ranch, Ozona, Texas.

I like this outfit. We get up in the morning, the girls cook breakfast. We catch our horses, ride off, and the girls wash the dishes, catch their horses, and trot to catch up. Then we work cows all morning, come in and take a nap while the girls cook dinner. Then we catch our horses and ride off, while the girls wash the dishes, catch their horses, and trot to catch up.

BILL DUGAN, *Cowboy*
Nye, Montana

I guess I catch more flack from old-timers than anyone else. The ranching tradition doesn't quite go hand-in-hand with a lady shoeing horses. Since it is such hard work, I guess the challenge of doing it motivated me to try to learn.

JOY SCOTT, *Lady horseshoer*
Alpine, Texas

My mother tried to give us some kind of refinement because the part that Daddy taught us was the rough end. I'm from the country but that doesn't mean we have to act like somebody without intelligence.

TOM MOORHOUSE, *Rancher*
Moorhouse Ranch Company
Benjamin, Texas

I was born in 1930, so I guess that arithmetic tells us I'm fifty-five. It might not look like it, but I've been riding since I was eight years old. I was breaking horses, as so-called, probably when I was fourteen. I didn't really ride that many tough colts. My father kind of took care of me and made sure that I didn't get into too much trouble. I guess that's because I was the only girl out of three other brothers, and being the only girl and the youngest, he thought I needed a little help. I've always been competitive. I enjoyed it. My father always told me that I could do just as well as they could and had me believing it. So I would try to outshoot them, outwork them, outdrive them. Anything that I could do to keep up or be a little better than they were thrilled me.

I started training horses after I met Ray Hunt, around 1960. I can't say that I've ever ridden many tough, tough ones because I really broke easily and brittle bones got in my way. But I like to test them a little. I don't really enjoy getting bucked off, so, I suppose I'll reach down there the first thing and pet her, tell her it's okay and then take the consequences. I do realize that whenever you climb on one, you've got a chance of going off and when you get a little older, you kind of protect your body a little more than you did. Maybe just experience and the years going by helped me. Not that I'm too far yet, but I'm happy about it anyway.

WINNIE LATTA, *Rancher*
West Wind Ranch
Gustine, California

My buckaroo is the first fellow that I ever went with that I had respect for his handling of horses. Anybody else, I felt like I did a better job. He's the only one I ever considered marrying.

He's been pretty careful about always getting the kind of jobs where I could ride with him. I'd like to think it's because he likes to have me with him, but it might be because he knows how unhappy I would be otherwise. I'm not as capable as a lot of men are with ropes and things like that, but he can coach me and we can get done what needs to be done. If he has to rope something out on the range, he can tell me just what to do to stay out of a jackpot and to help him also. Sometimes it probably takes lots of patience on his part. But as far as knowing what cattle are going to do and how the mind of a horse works, I feel I'm capable of getting the job done. I don't mind the housework as long as I don't get left out of the outside.

When I was a kid, my whole desire was *go West*, get on a ranch. I finally made the big, brave break and a dude ranch was the only way I knew how to get started on a ranch. I proved my capabilities and finally did get a cow job. I guess it was maybe a few years later that I married my buckaroo and we went on from there. But I think if I had to be a housewife, I'd consider it lonely.

EDIE MUNSON, *Buckaroo's wife*
Fitzgerald Ranch
Mitchell, Oregon

My dad cowboyed all of his life, and I grew up on ranches in Arizona, Nevada and Texas. He ran the LS ranch for seven years, now he is leasing a ranch in northern New Mexico, running steers.

After I married we went to work on the ZX in Oregon about the time they canned Ray McLaughlin. We liked him, so we left too. Then we worked in Wyoming, then Texas, then moved to Oklahoma and broke horses for a year and a half. In Oregon they won't let the women down at the barns, but in Wyoming I always helped. I always helped my dad brand and ship and scatter bulls and everything. It was a little different after I married because I felt sort of funny going out with the cowboys and being R. W.'s wife. I always felt sort of unwanted, whereas when I was growing up and went with my dad, I just did it.

It didn't really matter. I didn't want to go to college. I don't like to travel, I'm kind of the homebody. I would eventually like to buy a little place and buy a few good horses and some cows. Just have a neat little home place, raise some kids. When I was growing up, I went to about fifteen different schools. My dad just loved to move around. My main deal is, I've just wanted to have a place to call home. I just want to do something for myself; I've always been just Jake Moore's daughter or R. W. Hampton's wife.

DENISE HAMPTON, *Cowboy's wife*
Capitan, New Mexico

184

Sonya Goddard, Dodge City, Kansas.

Most people who say they'd like to do this don't have the courage to pick up and leave. Anybody can live in the city, but it takes heart to do this.

SHARON BURCHAM, *Cowboy's wife*
Sand Creek Ranch
Big Sandy, Montana

Marcy Weston, Valdez, Alaska and Carla Nelson, Alpine, Texas.

CHAPTER SEVEN

THE NEXT GENERATION

*The kids and the colts and the calves, a circle
just beginning where it ends*

I'M NOT THE FIRST PERSON to make a circle photographing and documenting the cow-boy, nor will I be the last, nor will this be my last circle. The colts just now being weaned and branded will be the bridle horses pictured in the new books. The calves now sleeping beside a dependable old baby-sitter, who will keep them safe until their mothers come back to relieve her, will all grow up. The best heifer calves will be the old mossy horns hiding their calves in the brushiest Arizona canyon until some now-little Duane Reece finds their track. The best bull calves will be saved from the knife both at branding and the supper table to be loaded in a trailer on a three-year-old colt by Bryan Neubert's kid using gear by young makers like Brown, Schutte, and Black.

Bill Dugan's kid will be handling the reins of a big team of horses pulling Charles Goodnight's dream around, working cattle just like they've always been. Ramón Hartnett's grandson will be standing beside a chuck wagon, shaking a spoon at the rest of the world, telling them to get the hell out of his "kitchen." Some of today's little cowgirls will probably be watching out the window of some lonesome line camp wishing they could ride with the wagon instead of cook and be mommies.

Some of the new generation will have grown up lucky, with parents who taught them young. Others are playing video games right now in Houston or Chicago or New York or Mexico City or Andrew, Iowa. They'll have a lot to learn fast whenever their minds snap, but they'll make it. They'll be better horsemen than we are, because a rock dropped into

187

water just keeps making circles. Their cattle will handle better, their saddles and bits and rawhide will put ours in the shade. And they won't care if they don't have much money or many modern conveniences.

And their photographs and words . . . !

When my three boys were small, they weren't big enough to catch a calf. We only had a few to do at a time and they were small calves so we took plenty of time. I'd catch a calf by the head and give the riata to one of them. They'd hold it while I caught it by one hind foot. We soon found out they could ride forward and pull the calf in the direction of the fire and go on by to the right of the fire. If they had to get their horse over sideways, they weren't that experienced. I found out as long as they were going forward they could ride by the fire. I would come around behind, circling to the left, until we had the calf right up to the fire.

There are a lot of different ways to bring a big calf up to the fire without having to drag the calf and the fellow that is holding the rope tight on the other end. I've seen some good horses just give up pulling. There is a way to change ends to get a calf up to the fire. It's a lot better to bring the calf up by one hind foot, standing up, than to have it flattened out and have to drag it up to the fire from the other side of the corral. If they don't drag it on in, the crew is right out in the way of the others that are roping. If you don't know any different, then that is good enough. You'll get the job done any way, sooner or later. But if you'll lead them in with one back foot, usually slowly, you can bring them in standing up and it is a lot easier on the livestock. The head man, who is following, will get up close and kind of help pull them if necessary. Here in California the calves are bigger than in a lot of other places and it is real easy to take a calf up to the fire if you have somebody on the other end that knows what to do. You can bring them from way out across the corral. But now, if you go too fast, even by one hind foot, you can flatten them out before you get to the fire.

I learned something else from my boys one time. It's always a struggle, it seemed to me, up to a point, getting that rope on the front feet of a calf. I was never pleased with the way it went on when I was doing it. One day when we were branding some little calves, the boys were trying to get the loop over the calf's front feet before they made the loop big enough and while the calf was still struggling. So we stopped and talked things over. It seemed that after the calf struggled a little bit and stopped, it laid there plumb still for a few seconds, plenty of time to get that rope on the front feet. So the first thing they did was to make the loop big enough, and then set it right out over both feet. Then they reached down through the loop, grabbing the lower foot and turning it back, then taking up the slack with the

Shannon Martin, W. T. Waggoner Ranch, Electra, Texas.

other hand. If the calf struggled when they caught that foot it would be turned back and keep the loop from sliding off. When I saw how it worked, I couldn't hardly wait to get off and try it myself. And of course, it worked just slick as could be. But I've never seen anybody that didn't get the rope on the front feet one way or another.

BILL DORRANCE, *Horseman*
Dorrance Ranch
Salinas, California

You can't buy the kind of quality you can raise.

BOB EIDSON, *Rancher*
Cross HE Ranch
Lovington, New Mexico

Lance Lacy, 06 Ranch, Fort Davis, Texas.

My mom taught me school because we didn't want to go to Elko school. There was more kids and they've got other friends to play with. I don't. But I would probably have made friends anyway.

I like living on a ranch. There's hardly any cars going by. You get to ride horses and you get to play with dogs. I get scared only when my horse runs because every time he runs, he bucks a little bit and I fall off. I fell off twice. I was riding with my dad once and we were trotting along or galloping and there was a ditch and the horse jumped the ditch and I fell off. Dad said, "I'll go get the horse." The horse even ran on the highway and almost got loose but Dad got him and unsaddled him. I said, "Boy, I wish I could ride more." But we didn't. Then the last time I fell off, we were practicing for the rodeo. I was galloping and I fell off and hit my leg on a rock. I almost broke it, but I'm glad I didn't. I was just doing barrels and it jumped and I fell off. I said, "I'm never gonna ride a horse again!" But Mom said, "Cowboy rules are always that you have to hop on the horse again and get goin' again." And I said, "Oooookay." And I got back on the horse and I went and never got bucked off again. But probably I will again, someday.

SAGE MITCHELL, 7
Stake Ranch
Jiggs, Nevada

My dad bought some new work horses and we were going to drive them down the lane and feed our cows in the spring. We were hauling hay. We were going to go across a cattle guard and go up to a gate. The hitch thing broke and the trailer hit the horses and they started running and running down through the sagebrush. I fell off with a hay bale about two inches from me. Dad fell off the trailer trying to get the horses out of the fence. I got up and got in the truck with Grandma and we zoomed down there. I thought Dad was under the trailer getting run over. I was bawling and Grandma was going about a hundred thousand miles an hour. I was scared. My dad finally got the horses quieted down and went on and fed the cattle and said they did fine.

I like the horses sometimes and sometimes I hate them. Sometimes I like playing with the animals and chasing them. We got chickens, goats, pigs, geese, ducks, cows and horses. It teaches me all kinds of things. Kids that live in town don't know how to feed cows or use a knife or saddle a horse or ride a horse, start a tractor, drive a tractor and milk the goats. That's fun!

DUSTY FUNKHOUSER, 9
Gamble Ranch
Montello, Nevada

My horse's name is Princie. I ride him with reins. They are attached to me and the horse. I used to ride on work horses. When my mama was haying and the horses were pulling the buck rake, I used to sit on the work horse's back. I always rode Kate. I hung onto the hames. It was fun. Ginger, I used to ride her bareback but she's dorky. Sandy, he'd always get in the brush. He was always getting my hands all skinned up and my face. I couldn't keep him out of the trees up in the rocks. One time he got up under a tree that was real low and he scraped me off. So Dad sold him. He was a little pony. I like big horses better because they are faster.

CASSIE RENAE FUNKHOUSER, 6
Gamble Ranch
Montello, Nevada

I got a four-year-old boy that's going to show a horse Sunday in the Elko Fair reining. He knows how to get a cow out of the herd and kind of hold her a little bit. He's starting to be help, cowboying. It's the most frustrating damn thing in the world, trying to get a kid to get around something. The danged old milk cow will be standing right there in the yard and she's wanting to come in but you got to go get around her. And I'll tell you, if you didn't say something to him, he's liable to go right at her and take her back out in the field. Or what's bad is, if he takes after the old milk cow any old way, she's liable to get around *him* and come in anyway. So he thinks he can do that with any cow. It's hard to get kids to get around an animal, to the back of it and bring it to you. And he's like my wife or my dog, if you ever ruin the mental attitude, it takes the fun out of it for him. Who wants to be screamed at? You've just got to make it so it's fun and show him what to do. You may have to firm up a little bit to get him to listen, though.

BRYAN NEUBERT, *Buckaroo*
Robert R. Marvel Ranches
Lamoille, Nevada

We were going to go spend the night with Grandma and we wanted to ride, so we just saddled up the horses and rode to Grandma's. It's about eighteen miles. Jed, my brother, went with me. He's twelve. Jed opened the gates. I held his horse. We went on the highway so we didn't have to open so many gates. When we got to our grandma's house we put our horses up.

JODY MOORHOUSE, 9½
Moorhouse Ranch Company
Benjamin, Texas

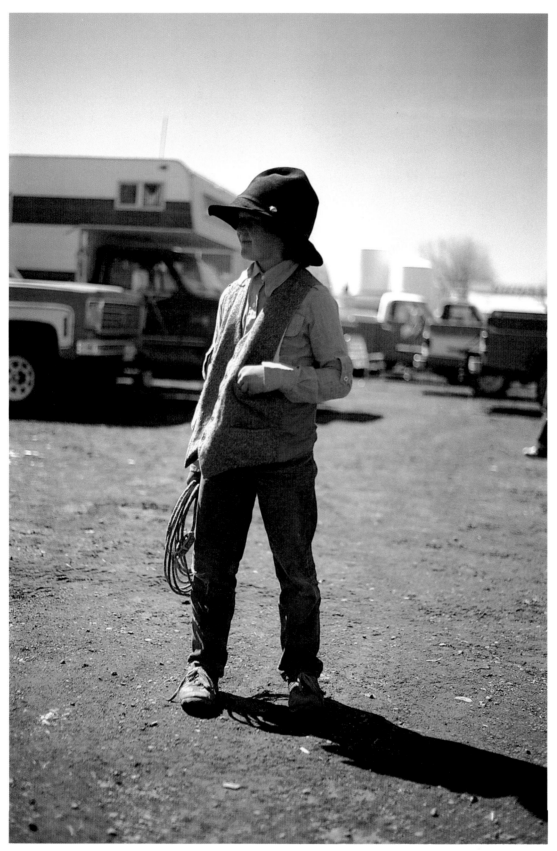

Noah Hall, Jordan Valley, Oregon.

You can learn just as much watching kids. Somebody that's real green, their problems will be real obvious. I might have the same problem, but it won't be as obvious to me because I've lived with it. But somebody else that has a problem—that's real obvious, you can see it. You can see what might correct it. If you can correct it with yourself, it's a lot easier that way. But a lot of people, they'll get around some guntzel that's having trouble all the time and they won't pay a bit of attention to him. If they would see what his problems are, they've probably got the same problems. Maybe not to that degree, but there's a good chance that somewhere they'll have a problem that's the same one this other fellow has. That's why I say you can learn a lot from kids.

MARTIN BLACK, *Buckaroo*
Gamble Ranch
Montello, Nevada

My favorite American Hero is the cowboy! The one that works on a ranch and doesn't get into fights all the time and doesn't go to the bar—much, anyway. My dad is a cowboy. Is your dad your American Hero? Mine is!

CARLA NELSON, 12
Alpine, Texas

All my kids help when we work cattle. Usually one of the older cowboys will take them under his wing and try to teach them something. I can't help but think it's a good experience for them. Someday they may have to do it whether they want to or not. One time we were gathering some steers off some lease land in South Texas. The steers broke right before we got them to the pens and ran off into the brush. The cowboys there couldn't catch my kids, they were in the lead. Whether you're involved in ranching in the U.S. or Mexico, you do so for the way of life, not the economic rewards.

ALBERTO MUZQUIZ, *Rancher*
Rancho la Rosita
Muzquiz, Coahuila, Mexico

I grew up on a small ranch in a nowhere place called Hasty, Colorado. I loved it. My horse, Risky, and I would go riding near every day. I took long walks over to my cousins' house where them and I would stack hay 'til late at night, or 'til it was too dark to see. Then we'd get on top of the stack and listen to the coyotes howling. Then we'd all jump in the pickup and go spotlighting. Even when my brother and I were riding fence, I loved it. In the middle of snowstorms I'd go out and stay with the horses, since the electricity was out anyway. I even got bowed legs already. If some things were different, I'd be back in Colorado right now, probably splitting wood or riding Risky through three-foot-deep snow, unless she had bucked me off. I was only half-done breaking her when I had to leave. One day soon, I'm going back for good.

TAMMY JO SMITH, 16
Seattle, Washington

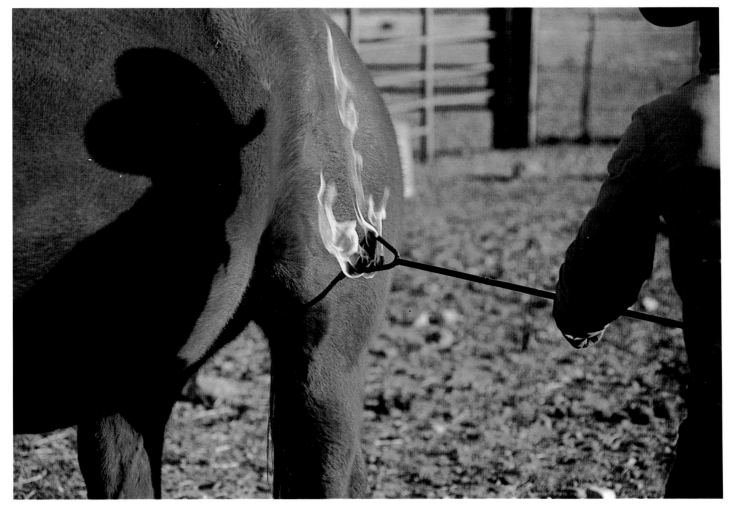

Colt branding, 06 Ranch, Alpine, Texas.

196   *Alberto Ecay Muzquiz II, Muzquiz, Rancho La Rosita, Coahuila, Mexico.*

Well, I probably can't ride him, but at least nobody can say I didn't try.

AUGUST LARSON, *Young buckaroo*
MC Ranch
Adel, Oregon

Tommi Jo had a sure-enough wreck early this summer with her horse. We had some first- and second-calf heifers get mixed up in two thousand acres of pasture near the river. We rode and sorted for three days. We had to pair cows and calves up simply by sittin' back and watchin' who sucked who, a slow process. Finished up late the third day and got off to shut the last gate. Sis crawled up on her horse while Tom held the reins. He then flipped them over the horse's head, but the wind caught 'em. Away Sam went hell bent for election, and Tommi Jo with no reins. I took after her (wrong) thinkin' maybe I could grab the reins or bump his shoulder to slow him down. 'Bout the time Tom got up 'longside, Sam really went full bore and Sis tryed to grab his halter and got strung out and off she went at breakneck speed. Man, did she take a tumble! Honestly thought that she would never move. Looked as though she popped her neck, but by danged she raised her head up and said, "Mom, I'm okay!" Talk about scared! She sure was a mess, as she slid on her face in the cactus. We pulled cactus out of her head for two months afterwards. Her eyes swelled shut and she had some scratches but wasn't even stiff the next day. She was back ridin' the next week and loves it. She's runnin' an old barrel horse this summer and plans to ride in the Labor Day rodeo. Her brother Trav sure would like to do some ropin' too, but time and money are two things we don't have.

JO CASTEEL, *Rancher*
TC Outfit
Vale, South Dakota

I'll probably stay here most of my life, I guess. I won't go to college, I know that. There's just nothing else I want to do.

MARK MCLAIN, 16
Whereabouts unknown

197

Cash Dugan, Nye, Montana.

Wilson Capron and dad, Mike, Fort Davis, Texas.

The babysitter, Cross HE calves, Lovington, New Mexico.

Clint McCloy, Pitchfork Land and Cattle Company, Guthrie, Texas.

When my son, Don, was a kid, he smelled catclaw blooming one time and said, "Dad, I feel that I'm breathing air that's never been breathed before!"

CURTIS LATIMER, *Rancher*
Colorado City, Texas

200

A two-year-old horse is about like an eight-year-old kid: you can sure sour him awful easy. It takes a while for him to get accustomed to work.

TOMMY VAUGHN, *Cowboy*
Leoncita Ranch
Alpine, Texas

I was taught to ride a pitching horse with a rein in each hand and not pull leather, but not everybody rides like I do. I kind of fudge a little. Oh, I'll go for some bronc rides and I may have to get back on one once in a while. But if I leave his head alone and don't pull on him, chances are he'll get it out of his system—get his head up where it belongs and go on. The first saddle, I don't care where he moves, he can go anywhere in any direction, if he'll just move. Most colts are either going to run, freeze up, or pitch; you can count on one of the three. Whatever they're going to do, I like to get it over with and move out. You've got to relax on a horse. If you're sitting there all drawed up waiting for him to blow up or something, when he does, you're so stiff he'll buck you off. You got to be ready, but you got to be loose. And if you're loose and relaxed, pretty soon the colt will go to getting loose and relaxed.

I control my temper the best I can. I call all of them dirty names when there's nobody around, but the less you aggravate one, the better off you are. That is something a man's got to work at. A lot of people are born patient, but they got to train that patience a little bit, too. On colts, the minute you step on one until you get off, he's aggravating you someway or another. You are always trying to teach him something and he's not wanting to do it and it's easy to lose your self-control—especially after you get one going good and he does a little something wrong. If you get mad and jerk him or scare him somehow, that's the quickest way to break yourself of getting mad, because then you have to start all over. Every once in a while it doesn't hurt to rap one if he needs it, but you've got to know when. It's like with a little kid; the quieter you are with him, the better kid he'll make. A horse has got to have confidence in the rider to be a good horse. If he's leery and scared of the man on him, he won't perform.

DONNIE SLOVER, *Cowboy*
Paducah, Texas

201

THE RIM

Thunderhead is boiling over the rim.
Summer shower coming with the wind.
Saddle horse a'nickering for his friend.
Afternoon is over,
Shadows gettin' longer,
Pastures are getting green again.

Cool front acomin' over the rim.
Horses turnin' tails into the wind.
Just finished workin' Number Ten.
Shipper calves are counted,
Shorts are all branded,
Fall work is underway again.

Bad norther's howlin' down the rim.
Ain't been this cold in I don't know when.
Just pulled the saddle off my friend.
Chopped ice since sunup,
Temperature ain't come up,
Wood stove will shore feel good again.

March winds are tearin' at the rim.
Been puttin' bulls out with the men.
'Bout tore our hats off by the brim.
Eatin' dust and gravel,
To help the outfit's cattle
Spring works astartin' up again.

Me n' her are sittin' on the rim.
Grama grass is hissin' in the wind.
City folks could never understand
People of the saddle,
Big land n' cattle.
Circle's just beginnin' when it ends.

Thunderhead is boiling over the rim.

JOEL NELSON, *Cowboy*
o6 Ranch
Alpine, Texas

Joel Nelson and daughter, Carla, on the rim, 06 Ranch, Alpine, Texas.

VOICES AND VISIONS
OF THE
AMERICAN WEST

has been set in Goudy Old Style type
by G&S Typesetters,
printed and bound by Dai Nippon Printing Co., Japan,
and designed by
Whitehead & Whitehead.